GREAT IDEAS FOR
MAKING MONEY

The Daily Express Guides

The Daily Express and Kogan Page have joined forces to publish a series of practical guides offering no-nonsense advice on a wide range of financial, legal and business topics.

Whether you want to manage your money better, make more money, get a new business idea off the ground – and make sure it's legal – there's a Daily Express Guide for you.

Titles published so far are:

Great Ideas for Making Money
Niki Chesworth

Your Money
How to Make the Most of it
Niki Chesworth

You and the Law
A Simple Guide to All Your Legal Problems
Susan Singleton

How to Cut Your Tax Bill Without Breaking the Law
Grant Thornton, Chartered Accountants

Be Your Own Boss
How to Set Up a Successful Small Business
David McMullan

Readymade Business Letters That Get Results
Jim Douglas

Available from all good bookshops, or to obtain further information please contact the publishers at the address below:

Kogan Page Ltd
120 Pentonville Rd
LONDON N1 9JN
Tel: 071-278 0433
Fax: 071-837 6348

Daily Express

GREAT IDEAS FOR MAKING MONEY

NIKI CHESWORTH

KOGAN
PAGE

First published in 1994

Kogan Page Limited
120 Pentonville Road
London N1 9JN
© Niki Chesworth and Express Newspapers plc, 1994

British Library Cataloguing in Publication Data
A CIP record for this book is available from the British Library.

ISBN 0 7494 1188 0

Typeset by Saxon Graphics Ltd, Derby
Printed in England by Clays Ltd, St Ives plc

Contents

Introduction

The ending of the recession marks an ideal time for anyone with entre-preneurial skills to go out and make money.

Millions of people have been hit by economic hardship—they are either unemployed or have seen their wages drastically reduced because of the slump.

Others simply want to better themselves by going it alone or mak-ing a few extra pounds on the side.

And then there are those who are trapped in jobs they no longer find challenging or rewarding, but there are few opportunities to move on to better jobs in pastures new.

If you fit into one of these categories, this book is for you.

The aim of 'Great Ideas For Making Money' is to spark off your interest in a money-making venture, to help you assess whether you are suitable to enter that type of business and to guide you through the opportunities and pitfalls.

The book not only looks at the earnings potential of different money-making ideas, but also at the costs involved, the risks and the sorts of skills you will need.

There are thousands of different companies in the UK and some three million self-employed so every business idea cannot be covered in just one book. It would take an encyclopaedia to assess each one.

Instead this book concentrates on money-making ideas that can be easily attained by anyone with the right skills, personality and dedication.

It will show you how to make the most of what you have. How to use your talents to make money, how to use your existing assets—from your home to your car and computer—to make cash, and where to go for further information and advice.

Before reading the ideas section it is essential that you read the pre-liminary chapters.

If you don't you could end up losing money instead of making it.

Part I

Guide Points to Running a Business

Is a money spinning idea for you?

Not everyone has what it takes to set up a business venture. While reading on, be realistic.

Can you organise yourself and your time? Are you tough enough to cope with difficult people like bank managers? Will you be able to negotiate with suppliers to make sure you are getting the best deal? Are you prepared to work hard and persevere? Most of all, do you really want to make money?

If all you want to do is make a quick buck, then you will probably be disappointed — or worse, be ripped off. Very few people make money easily, for most it is a case of hard work and more hard work.

Warning

Sharks are preying on the thousands of people, just like you, who are looking to make money. They may promise a £30,000 or even £50,000 income in their advertisements. They often say, high rewards for minimum outlay. And they always make it look easy. More often than not it is these people who make the money, not you.

Always check out any business venture thoroughly and never part with large sums of cash on the promise that you will be making a fortune in no time at all. Question why they want to make you rich. Surely they would be making a million for themselves, not someone else.

What you need to know about yourself

The first, and most important question you have to ask yourself is: Do you have what it takes to make money for and by yourself — without the security of a corporate umbrella?

You may not be planning to set up your own company just yet, but even if you are self-employed only on a part-time basis, you must remember you are ultimately responsible. If you fail it is down to you.

There are thousands of jobs to be done and plenty of opportunities—some lucrative, others more modest—if you have the application. It is not just your determination to succeed that counts, you must also pick a venture that suits your personality. There is no point in setting up a business from home if you lack self-motivation or need to work with other people. Similarly, if you find it hard to approach strangers, avoid anything that involves sales.

Personality

You need to ask yourself a number of questions about being freelance or self-employed:

- Can you cope with the stress of working alone?
- Are you prepared to work long hours in order to earn enough?
- Can you afford to take the risks associated with being your own boss?
- Are you self-motivated, or do you need someone else to push you along?
- Are you competitive enough to survive in the harsh world of business?
- Are you clear-thinking or do you panic in a crisis?
- Are you confident enough to stand on your own two feet?
- Are you resilient enough to keep going even when times get tough?

You may not think these qualities are essential, particularly if all you are planning to do is to turn your hobby into a money-spinner or let out a room in your house. But at the end of the day, whatever your venture, you will still need to sort out accounts and tax, deal with your bank, sell what you are offering and ensure that you make a profit.

If you are starting a business or becoming self-employed on a full-time basis it is even more important that you have got what it takes.

Ask yourself:

- Are you prepared to take risks if you need to?
- Can you accept failure and uncertainty?
- Can you manage your finances properly?
- Are you willing to accept a low income at first?
- If you have a family are they, and in particular, your partner, in favour of your going it alone?
- Can you accept the responsibility?
- Do you really know what you are letting yourself in for?

Skills

After asking yourself whether you have what it takes and whether you have the right personality, you should then analyse your skills—and your weaknesses. Be brutally honest. A few hours of deep thought now could save months of heartache later.

The type of money-making venture you choose should suit your personality and skills. It is also advisable to pick something you enjoy doing and know a bit about. For instance, if you have spent years as a local government planning officer, or as an executive in a large private

PROFESSIONALISM IN THE PEOPLE BUSINESS "ALL YOU NEED TO KNOW"

For many suitably experienced readers the acquisition of this business opportunity will be their entry into the Human Resources profession - enabling them to develop a lucrative and challenging business as a Consultant involved in all aspects of Careers, recruitment and training.

Throughout Britain more than two billion pounds turnover is generated each year by employment agencies and recruitment consultancies - with an estimated £100 million being generated by the developing **Career Counselling and Outplacement Consultancies** .... and a similar figure again by the **"Interim Management"** or **"Executive Leasing"** service providers.

The programme provides purchasers with all they need to successfully enter the Human Resource profession either in a full time or part time arrangement and with specially developed operating and marketing methods enabling the business to be promoted from your home.

The programme provides initial high quality training for 3 days - focussing on Interviewing skills, Marketing and Counselling - with specialist attention to C.V. preparation and the provision of a recognised "Personality Analysis Profiling" system - confidential sessions in book-keeping and business developments provided for those needing such help and professional video training films help with some of the modules such as networking, time management, body language etc.

All purchasers of the programme are supplied with a wide range of professionally produced booklets, pamphlets and leaflets .... not only for their own use but also to provide to candidates enrolling on their programmes when they start their own local businesses.

Purchasers are also provided with videos to support in the initial planning and the considerable input in the marketing and launching of each new business is helped by the provision of a Database of leading local employers and Sales promotional material.

The programme has many of the approaches normally associated with franchise schemes - but it is **NOT** a franchise.

Each purchaser of the business opportunity will be the owner of his or her own independent business and other than the initial purchase price **NO** other royalties, renewals or other payments are required.

Purchasers of the programme are expected to adhere to the principles of a special 'Code of Conduct' designed to ensure that best standards of professionalism are maintained .... and the acquisition of the programmes includes the option, if required, to use the name and logo.

Each purchaser of the programme is guaranteed the exclusive rights to use the programmes in their own immediate area - normally within their Parliamentary constituency and when each new business is ready to open a member of the team will spend a further day in each local purchasers area to help with detailed launch planning.

The business opportunity is based on twenty years successful experience in the professional recruitment and career counselling business enterprises - the author of the programmes Mr Arthur Flitter is a Fellow of the Institute of Employment Consultants and a qualified Accountant .... he heads up a highly skilled management team which develops the programme and provides the training.

The claim of the team is that purchasers of the programme are provided with **"ALL YOU NEED TO KNOW"**.

One important point to consider is that large sums of capital are not needed - a few hundred pounds of working capital to promote the new business should provide the start of a self financing and growing new business.

Whether you want a full time or part time business .... either on your own or perhaps in a partnership arrangement the business opportunity will enable you to join a sophisticated, established and developing profession - enabling you to be operational from day one!

AMBERLEY CONSULTANCY SERVICES LTD
Amberley House, 37 George Street, Staines, Middx., TW18 4LB
Tel: 0784 462131 or 463530   Fax: 0784 460197

firm or public enterprise, you could become a consultant selling the knowledge and expertise you have developed. Or, if everyone asks you to bake their cakes for weddings and Christmas—and you enjoy doing it—why not capitalise on what you know you are good at?

Remembering that your personality (particularly if you are outgoing) should also be considered as a skill, make a check list of the following:

- Qualifications—you should always make the most of these.
- Training—if you have trained for something, it is worth putting your talents to good use.
- Experience—setting up on your own is never easy, so make the most of what you know already. Moving into a new field is much harder than sticking to something you know lots about.
- What you enjoy doing—for instance DIY, cooking, meeting new people. If you enjoy your work, the chances are that you will be far more successful.
- Things you have been praised for at work or by friends—your hand-knitted jumpers, leadership or organisational skills, or your wheeler-dealer negotiating skills. If other people think you are good at something and have said so, then others will too.
- Other skills — don't forget to include your driving licence, your ability to type, the fact that you can use a knitting or sewing machine, or your green fingers.

Failings

Nobody is perfect so don't be afraid to admit that you are not good at something. It is far better to think about your failings now rather than when you fail later. Think about the following:

- Lack of skill—if you know nothing about what you are going into, own up now. Either avoid it or get training.
- Lack of business experience—again, you can go on courses to learn how to run a firm.
- Useless with figures—either get someone else (such as your partner) to keep on top of your money situation or learn about how to set up an efficient accounting system.
- Don't like selling—being a salesperson does not suit everyone. But at the end of the day you will be selling something, either a good or service or yourself. You may have a brilliant product or be the best in your field, but if you cannot convince others of that, you

risk instant failure. If you cannot master the art, consider employing an agent or someone else to do the selling for you.

- Don't get on well with other people—then consider working alone or from home.
- Frightened of taking a risk—again this can be overcome. You don't have to put your house on the line and invest your life savings in a business venture, you can start small and let it grow slowly.
- Don't want the responsibility of running my own firm—if this is the case then consider working as a self-employed agent of another company, temping for firms on a freelance basis or joining a network or multi-level marketing organisation. But at the end of the day, if you fail to find work or make money, remember it is down to you.

How to pick a business idea

You should now have a good idea of whether or not you have what it takes to set up a money-making venture, where your skills and weaknesses lie, and what personality traits you have that will help you succeed.

Now comes the hard part. What type of business can you turn into a money-spinner? Look at anything you have already that you can make money from.

Time

The old saying 'time is money' is certainly true. If you have plenty of time on your hands make the most of it. You may be retired, unemployed, working part-time, looking after a family, or have plenty of free time at the weekends or evenings. If so, there are many golden opportunities.

Two things you could consider are:

Selling your time to those who don't have much time to do things for themselves. This could be anything from offering a laundry service, walking someone's dog, acting as a secretary/answering service, setting up as a childminder, or to operating a delivery service. Those who are too busy to do something themselves or who need to free up their time for other things, will be prepared to pay someone else to help them out.

Mail Boxes Etc.(MBE), the worlds largest network of Postal, Business and Communication Centres, has over 2,000 of their unique franchised retail outlets in 11 countries.

This high street revolution offers 'One-Stop-Shop' convenience and flexibilty to local residents and businesses. As a Postal Alternative an MBE Centre Provides all the Royal Mail Products and Services excepting registered Mail. There are no queues, no bars and an MBE customer can expect to receive friendly and efficient service. With facilities to send and recieve Faxes, Photocopying, Personalised Mailbox Services, Stationery, Business services such as Printing, Word processing, Laminating and Binding, Mail Boxes Etc. caters for all those essential needs.

In association with The Royal Mail, Parcel Force, UPS, TNT, DHL, Federal Express and other recognised carriers, MBE are confident that they can get any package, anywhere at any time and probably do it cheaper. They also provide custom packing and packaging supplies.

All franchisees have the option to add on any products and services which enhance their image as a Postal, Business and Communication provider, depending upon their own abilities and the market in which they operate. Examples of which include instant signs, accountancy services, Rubber Stamps and Engraving, Secretarial Services, Company Formation & Registration, Gift Wrapping and Greeting Cards, Phone-messaging, Etc. Etc. Etc.

Computers UK Ltd

10 Furlong Road
Bourne End
Bucks
SL8 5DG

Tel: 0628 531876
Fax: 0628 531666

Second, turn your free hours to your advantage. If you tend to be free in the evenings or weekends, you should look at business opportunities that pay well due to the unsocial hours, or can fit round your other commitments. These can include anything from crafts to party-planning and direct selling (after all, most people are at home during these hours making them much easier to target).

Your home

This too can be turned into a business opportunity. It is probably your biggest asset, but also your biggest expense. Either turn a spare room into an office, your kitchen into a catering empire or your garage into a warehouse. Also consider taking in a lodger, offering bed and breakfast, or earning extra cash by looking after foreign students.

Starting a business from home saves on the expense of finding an office. Part of the running expenses can also be offset against tax. But watch out for the pitfalls. If you work from home you cannot get away from work, it is lurking there all the time. If you have a noisy family, you may be distracted. And always check with your household insurer because business equipment may not be covered under your policy, your local planning department and your mortgage lender first.

Your car

This, like your house, can be an asset and an major financial headache. However, it too can be turned into a means of making money as well as your ability to drive. It does not have to be a case of moonlighting as a minicab driver, you can set yourself up as a home delivery service, a courier, or even a chauffeur.

Your computer/telephone/fax

If you have office-type equipment at home, not only can you save money when going it alone, you can also use it to make money. Anything from offering a secretarial or typing service to more advanced computer skills can be offered.

Other assets

Your kitchen, DIY tools, gardening equipment can all be put to good use if you decide to turn one of your hobbies into a money-spinner.

Hobbies

Your hobbies prove you have an interest—and usually a skill—in something whether it be sewing, carpentry, cooking or playing the piano. These can all be put to good use.

What form should your venture take?

Whether you are working part-time or full-time you will generally have to become self-employed even if only for part of your earnings. You could also consider setting up a company.

Temping

This is the easiest way to make money out of your skills or time, whether it be spending your evenings as a silver service waitress or your spare hours as a typist. Headaches are kept to a minimum. Generally the employment agency will sort out payment and tax. However, you will still need to fill in a tax return at the end of the year.

Self-employed

If you are earning money in addition to your salary from your employer, or are intending to work full-time for yourself, you will need to have a self-employed tax status. You do not have to register as a company, but you will need to tell the Inland Revenue and Social Security of your new situation. This will enable you to reclaim expenses and costs against tax. Most new and small firms only need to submit simple accounts to the Inland Revenue.

You can usually fill in your tax return yourself, however it may be advisable to contact an accountant to ensure you are getting the maximum tax breaks. You should also find Inland Revenue leaflets very helpful.

Sole trader

You must then decide if you are going to set up alone, or with others. Most small businesses are one-person operations. However, as a sole trader you are completely responsible for any liabilities you incur in your business, which means your personal as well as business assets may be at risk.

Partnership

If you plan to set up in business with one or more others, you can become a partnership. This shares many of the characteristics of being a sole trader. It is simple to establish. Although you do not have to register a partnership formally, it is very strongly advised that you draw up a partnership agreement with the help of a solicitor. This will ensure that if anything goes wrong you are protected. It will also establish who has put what into the business, how the profits will be split, who does what work and what happens if the business is wound up. However, everything is at stake in a partnership — each partner is personally liable for all the debts incurred by the business. So if your partner(s) are not trustworthy you could be left with all the debts.

Oasis Computers Ltd have been active in the computer industry for the best part of a decade, firstly as conventional computer dealers and more recently as computer manufacturers.

Based in the heart of Somerset, their manufacturing plant produces a complete range of top quality computers with 100% industry standard compatibility. Each computer is carefully built to the customer's own exact specifications – no huge warehouses full of industry boxes waiting to be shifted here – and fully tested for 48 hours before despatch.

Every computer is supplied with a full 12 month parts and labour guarantee and a further lifetime warranty (labour only).

A full range of computers are supplied, from entry level 386SX's to the powerful 486DX2/66. A Pentium model is planned for 1994. In addition, Oasis produce a Multi Media Machine and also a range of business packages complete with computer, printer, software and a box of floppy disks!

For more information, please ring
OASIS COMPUTERS on **0458 835061**

Limited company

Many people starting up on their own or on a part-time basis do not bother to set up a limited company. However, it does not have to be expensive (you can buy one ready formed off-the-shelf) and it does have its advantages. Limited company status separates the company from its owners. As such you will not usually be personally liable for its debts because normally creditors can claim only on the assets of the business. However, you may still be required to give a personal guarantee on certain loans. There is also such a thing as director's liability — which can make a director personally liable if he or she allowed the firm to continue trading knowing that it was insolvent.

You will need to register your company, provide regular accounts and draw up articles of association.

Franchises

You may not have a brilliant business idea of your own, but still know that you have what it takes to run your own business. In this case, franchising may be the answer to your problems. You simply buy your business idea from an existing — and ideally — successful business. The likes of Perfect Pizza, Athena, Ryman and the Body Shop are all run on this basis.

And if you are not up to scratch, you could be in breach of your contract and have your franchise taken away from you.

Multi-level marketing

This is another alternative to setting up your own firm. You act as an agent or distributor for a firm that only employs a direct sales staff and does not sell through high-street outlets. In theory this cuts out the middle-man, enables the products to be priced competitively and allows the agent to make a profit.

Business plans

If you don't want to work for others, then whether you work freelance, are self-employed or start a business, you need a business plan.

Why do you need a business plan?

- To raise finance
- To clarify and commit your business objectives, and short- and long-term plans, to paper.
- To test the viability of your business idea without risking/spending any money.
- To help decide on how to structure your new or existing business.
- To provide a set of objectives that can be used as a yardstick against which you can judge the performance of your venture once it is up and running.

What details should appear in the business plan?

Your business plan should be as brief as possible and easy to read. It should be a useful ready reckoner for you, and contain enough information for potential lenders and investors to comprehend at first glance. A well-presented business plan is as important to a sole-trader as it is to a major multinational.

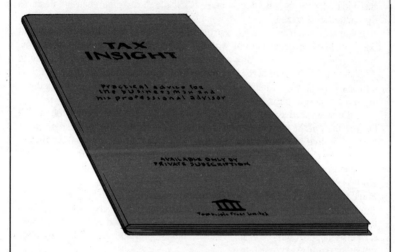

'YES'

Published by Context Communication Services Ltd. since 1992, 'YES' magazine is now widely regarded as the UK's Leading Business Opportunities Magazine. In full colour with over 70 A4 glossy pages packed cover to cover every month with up-to-date information and Topical Articles from some of the UK's leading writers and entrepreneurs, together with a full and varied range of affordable display and classified advertising, all goes to make 'YES' the most comprehensive Business Opportunities Magazine.

If you are already in business or promoting a business opportunity you will find 'YES' invaluable in providing YOU with the information to help your business grow and prosper. If you are seeking a business opportunity not only will you find in 'YES' details of hundreds of the leading business opportunities, but also a wealth of information and ideas to help YOU promote and build that opportunity into a thriving and prosperous business.

As the recognised leader in this field of publishing, 'YES' has become the Launch Pad for many of the most successful ideas and opportunities. Our dedicated team is perfectly poised to ensure that readers of 'YES' magazine are amongst the first to learn of any changes and developments which could influence your business and our extensive network of contacts, worldwide, enables us to ensure that 'YES' is always ON TOP!

More than just a business opportunities magazine...

More than just a Business Opportunities Magazine, 'YES' is also one of the UK's leading Business Opportunities. We offer both our Standard and Executive Subscribers an opportunity to earn a realistic and long term income whilst providing full support and every assistance.

As a Standard Subscriber (£24.95) we will provide you with 100 'YES' FREE SAMPLE COPY flyers to help get your promotion started, these flyers have been specifically designed to be included with, and to complement your existing mailing activities. We pay a £5 bonus for every subscriber introduced to 'YES' so after just 5 introductions you have the opportunity to automatically upgrade your subscription to the full Executive Subscription at no extra cost.

As an Executive Subscriber (£49.95), in addition to being eligible to receive a 15% discount on all advertising placed with 'YES' magazine, you also qualify for FREE ENTRY in the 'YES' Subscriber Network on which you will be eligible to receive commission payments down to five levels. To help get your promotion started we provide you with 100 'YES' FREE SAMPLE COPY flyers.

At both levels of Subscription we also provide you with an additional 100 flyers FREE OF CHARGE for every subscriber you introduce. The Subscriber whom you introduced will also receive 100 flyers FREE OF CHARGE, helping to get their promotion started and ensuring the continued growth of your business and the perpetuation of the Network.

...more than just a business opportunity

'YES' join the winning team!

To receive a FREE SAMPLE COPY of 'YES' magazine and full details on how you can build a realistic long term income write to:

'YES' Magazine – GMM
Unit 17, Telfords Yard, 6-8 The Highway, London E1 9BG

The plan should contain the following:

- Summary
- Introduction
- The identity of your business
- A description of the product or service
- The market it is aimed at
- The pricing policy
- Who owns it
- The date the business began
- The date of incorporation (when it was registered if it is a company)
- Where you operate from
- Number of employees (if more than just you)
- The legal basis of the business
- Who your main suppliers and customers are
- Management and CVs
- Risks
- Objectives

"WHERE THERE'S A WILL THERE'S A BUSINESS..."

With a market in excess of 26 million people without a Will, Legal Systems Limited has launched the first comprehensive automatic Willwriting software program in the country. It is the most sophisticated and user-friendly program now available and will run on any IBM compatible computer and printer.

The program is available on a low cost annual licence fee and comes with a superb built-in database which not only manages your business but also provides a unique marketing tool to maximise sales.

The database allows you access to other legal services including the Enduring Power of Attorney and the 'Living Will' each of which can provide the Practitioner with added fee income. More fees can be earned from probate and document storage, thus providing the Practitioner with long term renewal income. The company also provides one of the best conveyancing packages in the country.

There are four board directors of the company including a lawyer and a team of Regional Marketing Directors to help support Practitioners in their business development.

The company conducts quarterly workshops whereby all Practitioners can meet, exchange ideas and hear guest speakers from within and outside the profession to ensure continued success and motivation. The sales and marketing side of the business is second to none.

Full comprehensive training is provided and the package includes professional indemnity insurance. A 24 hour helpline with full legal and technical support is provided.

Legal Systems Limited   081-300 9333

- Plan of action
- Financial information
- A SWOT analysis. This covers strengths, weaknesses, opportunities and threats.

Will your idea make money?

There is no point in coming up with what you think is a brilliant idea to make money if you don't do the groundwork to ensure that it will work in practice. The questions you should ask yourself are these, as well as the research you need to do before going ahead:

Who will buy my product or service?

Target the market you are going for then test it. Find out if people really want or need your product or service and whether they are prepared to pay for it. Also check out the viability of your idea with your local Training and Enterprise Council or Enterprise Agency and your bank. And check out the competition.

Is there enough demand?

Once you have found out whether or not your idea is a good one, you then need to judge the demand for your goods or service. You could try a test marketing excercise by either ringing or writing to potential customers. Also find out how similar businesses in your chosen field are faring. Or if other people doing something similar to your plan are earning enough to keep them afloat.

What makes my product/service special?

However original your idea, someone somewhere is bound to have come up with something similar. To really succeed you need a USP — Unique Selling Point — which makes yours different or special and will persuade people to buy it for the price you are charging. Make the most of this special feature when marketing your business. It can be anything that makes your business, product or service special, from 24-hour opening to a money-back guarantee. For instance, if you make a food item, you can promote the fact that it is 'additive free' or 'baked on the premises'. If you offer a service, your USP may be your flat-rate pricing, opening hours or location. But remember, your USP will be a major selling tool so you must live up to promises. It is no good saying 'Never knowingly undersold' like the John Lewis stores if you are the most expensive shop in town.

What is the competition like?

Even if you think you have a viable business idea, once you check out the competition you may change your mind. If you are up against some very efficient and well-established firms you may not be able to beat them on price or better their service or quality.

What price will people be prepared to pay?

This is a hard one to answer. Until someone actually parts with cash you do not know what they will pay. However, by checking out the competition you will get an idea of the going rate. Don't be tempted to undercut the market too much — you may boost sales but make no profits.

Can I make a profit at that price?

You will need to look at costs and prices and ensure you have enough of a margin to cover your overheads, salary, business costs and marketing. You will only break even if your turnover reaches a certain level. Make sure that this is realistic.

Where should I set up my business?

The old saying 'location, location, location' certainly rings true for most businesses. If it is not the cost of premises, it is whether or not they are in the right position to attract passing trade or in the right neighbourhood to appeal to the sort of customers you are trying to attract. For most small firms, however, the answer will be at home. It is cheaper to start up without renting premises. However, if you do need a high street presence, location can make or break your business.

How to make the most of your bank and raise finance

Bank accounts

The first thing you will need before starting up is a bank account purely for your business. This makes it easier to keep track of your finances and also ensures that they do not get confused with other earnings or household bills.

Many sole traders go to their existing bank. As they know you already, it will probably be easier to set up an account and raise finance. However, if you are not satisfied with the service or do not get a positive response, shop around. Ask friends and other small businesses who they recommend.

To make the most of your banking relationship you should keep your bank fully informed of your progress. If you run into trouble, tell them immediately. If you don't, the bank will be worried about your future and could pull the rug from underneath you.

Remember you can usually negotiate terms and rates for loans and don't forget to check your bank statements.

Make the most of your bank manager's experience. He or she may have dealt with similar firms to your own and you can learn from others' mistakes. Also, make the most of literature and other services on offer.

Raising finance

The bank

Your first port of call will probably be your bank. If you want a loan, you will probably be required to put up some security — such as your home — to back the loan should you default.

You will need a business plan to prove why you need the money, and that the amount of money you have requested is enough to finance your venture. If you ask for too little, you may quickly run into financial difficulties.

Short-term finance can usually be arranged through an overdraft facility. Remember it is just a facility and can be removed. For longer term finance consider loans — particularly at fixed-rates to help with budgeting.

However, the bank is not your only port of call.

Venture capital

Venture capital is a medium- to long-term investment, not just of money, but also management time on behalf of the venture capital company.

Venture capital is often regarded (often unjustly) as the last resort when looking for capital. But a venture capital firm is looking for more than just a financial return; they are willing to contribute management time to the business (providing strategic advice) and to develop the business with you as an equity partner — they usually have a seat on the board. Venture capitalists take a risk on their capital as well.

Why venture capital? It is a means of financing the start-up, expansion, or purchase of a company. It is only worth approaching a venture capital firm if you don't mind their extremely close involvement in every aspect of your business and whether you fulfil their business criteria. They look for a company (and it can be small) with:

- A good product.
- A market where the company can gain a protected position.
- High margins.
- A management team with direct experience of the product and market.

Further information and a list of members can be obtained from:

For £299* you can be the most informed person in your company.

There's nothing like a company fax machine for keeping you well informed. And helping you respond to situations quickly.

However, getting things to and from it can often be frustrating.

Which is why Samsung has introduced the new SF500 fax/phone: a more convenient fax for your desk that provides a speedier, not to mention confidential, way of communicating with clients.

It incorporates an automatic fax/phone switch with a remote extension pick up facility, that is especially designed for home use.

There's a port for an answerphone. And, thanks

to a clever polling facility you can access informatio bureaus or call up other fax machines to reques stored information direct.

We've even included a Mercury access button t help keep running costs to a minimum.

Unbelievable as it may seem, the SF500 cost only £299* or £349* for the more advanced SF505 and both come with a free 12 months on site warrant

To find out more about how a Samsung fa could help you around the office, or at home, fi in the coupon.

After all, we wouldn't want you to make decision until you've been properly informed.

*PRICES EXCLUDE VAT.

FROM CORPORATE TO HOME ENVIRONMENT – SAMSUNG FAXES FIT THE BILL

Samsung Electronics is the third largest electronics company in the world and is renowned for its success in telecommunications, computing and consumer electronics. In addition, it is involved in almost every industry imaginable from shipbuilding to pharmaceuticals. Experience in a wide variety of markets has established the company's reputation for creating unique solutions suited to all business and domestic applications.

Samsung Electronics (UK) Ltd is the leading supplier of facsimile machines in the UK. This success is due to continued commitment to research and development and sourcing new technology to allow the company to respond to the needs of the user.

In a highly competitive market, Samsung has achieved its premier position in the fax market by addressing user demand from each end of the spectrum – from corporate to domestic.

The SF2500 Ansafax, aimed at the business professional combines the advanced technology of a sophisticated telephone answering system with the flexibility of a fully-featured fax machine. It distinguishes automatically between voice and fax, recording messages when the recipient is absent. It incorporates remote control technology which allows the user to retrieve messages and to control all other answerphone features remotely via any normal touch-tone 'phone. It also has a 10-page document feeder and 59 speed dial numbers for the busy executive. The SF2500 costs just £499 (+ VAT).

The SF1505 is next in the range and gives exceptional value at £399 (+ VAT). Like the SF2500 it includes paper cutter, 2 line LCD display and automatic fax/telephone switch together with an alpha memory search and dial function and ansaphone port.

For the small business user, Samsung has introduced the SF505 and SF500 at £349 and £299 (+ VAT) respectively. These machines provide some of the user-friendly devices of the higher end models, such as automatic fax/telephone switch which means that the user needs only one telephone socket for both 'phone and fax and extension pick up facility. Both machines have ansaphone ports for connection to an existing answering machine. The SF505 also has an LCD display for easy programming. Both models are PABX compatible with mute buttons and call transfer facilities.

Last but, by no means, least are Samsung's two new babies – the SF30 and SF40. The SF30 is specifically aimed at the domestic user, the SF30 measures just 13.3" × 8.3" × 3.1". Its aesthetic design means that it can blend in with any interior and can sit comfortably on a telephone table or in a small study. Incorporating fax/phone switch, 10-number speed dial facility and extension 'phone transfer, the SF30 costs just £249 (inc VAT).

The SF40 is the new executive desktop fax machine for the corporate executive with a requirement to send and receive confidential or sensitive information. The SF40 is priced at £299 (inc VAT).

On-hook dialling capabilities and a Mercury button are included on all models.

Samsung's reliability and credibility is a tangible result of a close partnership with its customers, listening to their needs and developing affordable products to exceed all expectations.

All machines are available from office equipment dealers and superstores except the SF30 which is exclusively available from leading multiple retailers including Dixons and Comet.

For a full list of stockists contact Lynda Aldworth at Samsung Electronics (UK) Ltd. Telephone: 081-391 0168.

The British Venture Capital Association
3 Catherine Place
London SW1EE 6DX
071-233 5212

You can also get two very useful free guides from The British Venture Capital Association (the association which represents venture capital companies and the industry): 'A Guide To Venture Capital' and 'Business Plans and Financing Proposals'.

Leasing and hire purchase

This is a way of spreading the cost of large items over a long period of time. However, remember, if you lease equipment you never become the owner of it. The advantage is that there is no large capital outlay so it can help cashflow. Vehicles are usually bought under contract hire, which is for a period set at less than the estimated life of the equipment. The financing deal may also include maintenance.

Hire purchase or credit sale means that you own the asset outright at the end of the hire period. These also have certain tax advantages as you can claim a capital allowance from the time you start using the equipment.

Factoring

This is a means of easing cashflow. You sell your debts to raise cash and get a certain percentage — up to 80 per cent — of the value of invoices. The balance — minus a factoring fee — is paid when the debts are collected. But you will generally need sales of around £100,000 a year to factor your debts.

Other sources of financial help

You should not overlook Government schemes and grants when looking for finance.

The Loan Guarantee Scheme

This is run by the Department of Trade and Industry and provides a guarantee for loans by banks and financial institutions to firms unable to obtain conventional loans because they lack security or a track record. A premium is paid by the borrower in return for a guarantee of the loan over a certain amount. Ask your bank manager for further details.

Enterprise Scheme

This scheme has changed although it is still referred to as the Enterprise Allowance. It is now much more flexible. If you have been unemployed you may qualify for help in setting up your business. This is a regular allowance paid over an agreed period of time. Sums vary from £20 to £90 a week for up to 66 weeks. Ask your local Training and Enterprise Council (TEC) or Job Centre for advice.

British Coal Enterprise Ltd

This provides help to businesses expanding or locating in coal mining areas and employing former British Coal employees. *Low-interest loans* or help in obtaining premises are provided. Tel: 0623 826 833.

British Steel Industry Ltd

This also offers assistance in traditional steel producing areas in the form of loan finance, training, and in certain areas managed workshops. Tel: 0742 731612.

Prince's Youth Business Trust

Grants and low-interest loans are available to young people starting a business. Tel: 071-321 6500.

The Rural Development Commission

A useful guide to the assistance available to businesses in rural areas of England from the Government and non-profit making agencies is published by this organisation. Tel: 0722 336 255.

Other grants/assistance

If you are in an Urban Programme Area or Assisted Area, or if your business idea is innovative or in a technological field, the Government has grants on offer. Your local Department of Trade and Industry office should be able to give you details of all these schemes. Lastly, local authorities can provide help to new businesses.

Selling your idea

Whatever business you are in you will need to sell — either your goods, services or yourself. So it is important to get your sales image right.

Name

This is vital to your image. The wrong name can make you look cheap, the right one can imply good value. It is not only your business that will need naming but also your goods and services. You will however, have to check with Companies House or the Patent Office that the name is not already in use.

Make sure your name reflects your special features, the location of your firm — if that is a selling point — and appeals to the types of customer you are trying to attract.

Invented words make good names but they may not be instantly recognisable if you are a new business. If you do use one, register it as a trademark.

Marketing

This is essential if you want to attract business quickly. You should not expect trade to come to you. It can take several forms:

Advertising

Always convey your key messages of price, service, quality, style and locality. Remember your advertisements will reflect your image, so it is worth investing in some good quality artwork. Target your adverts to your type of business and to the sort of customer you are trying to attract.

Public relations

This can be much cheaper than advertising especially if you do it yourself. It involves targeting media to write about or cover your product or service. The easiest place to start is your local newspaper. When you launch, send out a press release detailing in a punchy and concise form what you are doing. Limit your press release to two pages at the most. Alternatively you can host a press conference or open day and invite journalists along.

Direct mail

This involves sending out sales literature or letters to potential clients. Remember the quality of your catalogue, brochure, or letter will reflect the image of your firm. Try to target your mailshots to avoid wastage. At first use the *Yellow Pages* or other business directories to build up a mailing list. Then mailshot regular clients to ensure repeat business and build up customer loyalty.

Insurance

This is probably the last thing on your mind when setting up on your own. But without certain types of insurance you will be breaking the law. You also risk losing everything if your business burns down, or you have an accident and cannot continue to work.

Types of insurance you must have or should consider include:

- Employers' liability to cover against injury or accidents at work suffered by your employees.
- Motor insurance.
- Insurance needed by contracts.
- Insurance for certain types of equipment.
- Fire, flood and other perils cover.
- Insurance for loss of profits if your business suffers due to fire or other insured peril.
- Insurance against theft, loss of money.
- Cover for goods in transit.
- Credit insurance to protect against customers' failure to pay.
- Public liability and product liability — a good idea if you are in the service business.
- Professional indemnity if you are in a business where you could be sued for negligent advice.
- Legal expenses to cover you if you are in a legal wrangle.
- Income protection/keyman insurance to protect your firm's income should you or a key member of staff fall ill or die.
- Cover for computers and computer records, business machines and equipment — particularly if they are leased.

Accounts

Keeping track of your financial situation is vital when you are setting up on your own. However small your business venture, you will need to know your costs and your income exactly to ensure that you are making a profit and not in danger of running into financial problems.

Accounts procedures

You will need to keep accurate records of your income and expenditure. This is not only essential for your own information but so that you can submit your accounts for tax purposes.

Tax

It is important that you pay no more in tax than you need. It is also vital that you keep on top of your tax affairs. An unexpected tax bill could drive you under. The self-employed will pay income tax on profits minus justifiable expenses and allowances. Businesses face Corporation Tax. Later on you will need to consider Capital Gains Tax and possibly Inheritance Tax. If you set yourself up as a director of a limited company you will pay income tax on your salary at normal rates with profits left in the business liable for Corporation Tax.

National Insurance

You will also have to pay National Insurance contributions if you become self-employed on a full-time basis. Check with your local Social Security Office.

VAT

You must register your business for VAT if you expect your turnover to exceed the threshold set in the Budget which is £45,000. Not everything is subject to the maximum rate of VAT. You will need to know which VAT regulations relate to your business.

There has been much talk in recent years of communications technology creating more home based employment but it is still difficult to find specific examples. An interesting business opportunity that exploits this concept is a low-cost franchise package offered by Assured Travel Limited. If you are interested in the world of travel and you are prepared to risk £1,350.00 in start-up costs you are in business almost overnight.

The franchise exploits the concept of a central database/administrative hub that you can access via a modem link 24-hours a day. A particularly interesting feature is that no fixed operating costs are imposed on the franchisee network. The business has a hint of a global family operation about it. Well worth contacting them for an information pack (without any obligation on your part). If you find you are genuinely interested you can take a few soundings with some existing franchisees and you are encouraged to visit their offices in Bedford.

In addition to supplying everything you need to operate in the market they also run a two-day residential introductory training programme. Thereafter several permanent staff provide the back-up. Your main risk would appear to be that for whatever reason you are unable to evolve and develop a client base and dig out the bookings. Probably best suited to those with administrative/sales/computer backgrounds.

Part II

The A–To–Z of Great Ideas for Making Money

ALTERNATIVE/COMPLEMENTARY MEDICINE

It's always easy to make money out of any new fashion or fad. Although alternative medicine (also known as complementary medicine) is not new, it is now much more popular due to royal interest — Prince Charles for example — and it is gaining credence.

Many people have become frustrated with conventional medicine and have lost faith in its powers — they don't see that drugs and surgery are always the solutions to their medical problems — and so have opted to give the more natural complementary medicine disciplines a try.

Unlike traditional medicine it does not generally require lengthy training, and courses can be taken by almost anyone with an aptitude and an interest. Although areas like acupuncture and homeopathy require a high degree of skill, others like aromatherapy can be practised by almost anyone.

What is complementary medicine?

Complementary medicine treats the whole person (holism). Ancient and traditional methods of health care concentrated as much on the causes of illness as on the effects, and as such the treatments were designed to stimulate self-healing and reduce pain or the distress of symptoms.

Traditional medicine works on the principle that one is healthy when body, mind and vitality are in balance. Complementary medicine helps to restore the correct balance. It helps with back pain, muscular pain, headaches, skin conditions, dietary problems, and depression and emotional problems. The most common forms of complementary medical disciplines are acupuncture, homeopathy, reflexology, massage, aromatherapy, osteopathy and chiropractic.

As well as physical treatments, other complementary treatments are available to help the mental and emotional condition by calming the mind and helping to remove distressing symptoms. These treatments include hypnotherapy, counselling, meditation, and relaxation techniques.

Counselling

Counselling helps relieve mental disorders, stress and anxiety by listening to the problems of the patient and helping them to unburden their fears, worries and past traumas and to come to terms with them. Counsellors are trained to listen without becoming emotionally involved. There are several organisations that train potential counsellors. For more information contact:

The British Association of Psychotherapists
37 Mapesbury Road
London
NW2 4HJ
081-452 9823

The British Association for Counselling
1 Regents Place
Rugby
Warwickshire
CV21 2PJ
0788 578328

Are you suitable?

You must have a genuine interest in your chosen field and be prepared to deal with things medical. You have to be prepared to visit people in their homes and have the right manner — be sympathetic and look the part. People don't want to be 'treated' by a scruffy-looking individual who looks unhealthy and unkempt (that's hardly reassuring).

Qualifications and training

This is a must. You will have to contact the appropriate body that represents your particular field. You will generally need to pay for the courses yourself as you rarely get grants for this type of work.

Once you have done your initial training you need to get a good number of hours of work behind you. You should do evening or weekend work to fit your new skill round other work you do.

Costs

The initial outlay is basically the time spent learning your skill and marketing yourself, plus any equipment that you might have to buy when you start your own business.

How much can you make?

This all depends on which discipline you go in for and how popular that is.

Where to find more information

The British Holistic Medical Association's (BHMA) areas of participation cover self-hypnosis and hypnotherapy, relaxation and stress management, spirituality, meditation, which all help patients through times of illness and distress:

British Holistic Medical Association
179 Gloucester Place
London NW1
071-262 5299

The Council for Complementary and Alternative Medicine (CCAM) is a forum for determining standards of education, training, qualification, ethics and discipline for practitioners of complementary and alternative medicine. The CCAM represents organisations and practitioners in the following complementary medicines: acupuncture, osteopathy, medical herbalism, homeopathy, and naturopathy.

The Council of Complementary and Alternative Medicine
179 Gloucester Place
London
NW1 6DX
071-724 9103

The Institute of Complementary Medicine (ICM) acts as a 'clearing house' and register of all disciplines of alternative and complementary medicine. The ICM produces a very useful pamphlet as an introduction to complementary medicine.

Institute of Complementary Medicine
21 Portland Place
London W1
071-237 5165/5175

Shiatsu

This is Japanese 'finger pressure therapy' — a natural healing discipline springing from the same ancient oriental principles as acupuncture. It is used to relieve stress and put the receiver more in touch with his or her own body's healing abilities.

No formal qualifications are required. But you should have a degree of physical suppleness. However, training for a qualification as a professional shiatsu practitioner takes 500 hours of study.

Where to find more information

Shiatsu Society
5 Foxcote
Wokingham
Berks
RG11 3PG
0734 730836

Aromatherapy

Aromatherapy is the ancient art of healing through the use of essential oils — oils that are extracted from plants, leaves, twigs, fruits, and other vegetable matter. These can be used to treat specific problems, from headaches and depression to problems of the skin and nervous system. Qualifications are not mandatory but you can get training.

Where to find more information

Tisserand Institute
65 Church Road
Hove
West Sussex
BNA 3XA
0273 206640

Chiropractic

Chiropractic is the treatment of neuro-musculoskeletal disorders, particularly in the spine and pelvis to relieve those areas of pain. You need higher qualifications to practise.

Where to find more information

British Chiropractory Association
29 Whitley Street
Reading
Berks RG2 0UG
0734 757557

Reflexology

Reflexology, which has an affinity with acupuncture, is a natural healing science based on applying pressure to minute points in the feet, which then stimulates the whole body to tackle various ills such as migraine, asthma, blood pressure and so on. Anyone can practise reflexology, although you can do a course at the British School of Reflexology to become a qualified member.

British School of Reflexology
The Holistic Healing Centre
92 Sheering Road
Old Harlow
Essex CN17 0JW
0279 429060

Osteopathy

Osteopathy is the system of diagnosis and treatment that concentrates mainly on the structural and mechanical problems of the body, and uses the combination of the oldest forms of treatments — massage and manipulation.

Osteopathy helps to re-align structural deviations and abnormalities particularly of the spinal cord, but also of other structures. Osteopathic treatment can remove tension, restore normal movements of the body as a whole and reduce any irritations of the nervous system, circulation problems, and swellings.

As the law stands at present anyone in the UK can call himself or herself an osteopath and open a practice without the need for any training at all.

Where to find more information

The General Council and Register of Osteopaths, and the Osteopaths Association of Great Britain are the two main bodies that regulate osteopaths.

The General Council and Register of Osteopaths
56 London Street
Reading
Berks RG1 4SQ
0734 576585

Osteopaths Association of Great Britain
206 Chesterton Road
Cambridge CB4 1NE
0223 359236

Medical herbalism (Phytotherapy)

Medical herbal remedies provide the trace elements, vitamins and medicinal substances in a harmonious (drug-free) way to restore health in patients.

Medical herbalists look beyond a patient's surface symptoms to evaluate the overall balance of a body's systems, to discover underlying disharmonies. Different remedies may be used to treat two patients suffering from the same ailment because the whole person is being treated, not the disease.

Where to find more information

National Institute of Medical Herbalism
9 Palace Gate
Exeter EX1 1JA
0392 426022

British Herbal Medicine Association
Field House
Lye Hole Lane
Redhill
Avon BS18 7TB
0202 433691

Acupuncture

Acupuncture is part of the traditional medicine of China and the Far East. Acupuncture uses fine needles to stimulate channels of energy running beneath the surface of the skin. This effects a change in the energy balance of the body to restore health. Each point that is used in acupuncture has a precise location and specific therapeutic action.

Acupuncture in the UK today is used to eliminate pain or for the treatment of obesity or smoking. But it is most effective for treating common diseases and conditions such as asthma, headaches, arthritis and rheumatism, menstrual disorders, skin complaints, and for anxiety and depression.

Where to find more information

Academy of Chinese Acupuncture
52 Calderon Road
London E11 4EU
081-558 7773

Council for Acupuncture
179 Gloucester Place
London NW1 6DX
071-724 5756

Homoeopathy

Homoeopathy is based on the principle of treating like with like. All symptoms are recognised by homoeopaths as expressions of disharmony within the whole person and so the patient rather than the disease is treated. To become a homoeopath, you do need qualifications.

Where to find more information

British Homoeopathic Association
27A Devonshire Street
London W1N 1RJ
071-935 2163

ANTIQUES DEALING

You have to be interested in antiques to want to be part of the scene and carve out a living in this very specialised area. The BBC's Antiques Roadshow may have whetted your appetite. Or perhaps TV's Lovejoy is a better role model for an antiques dealer? Did you know that comedian Ronnie Barker, from the Two Ronnies, is now an antiques dealer in his retirement? All sorts of people become antiques dealers.

Are you suitable?

Only consider becoming an antiques dealer if collecting antiques is a hobby of yours, or you have an interest in the subject. Above all, you need to know what you are doing, otherwise you could be 'conned' by experts who know the value of items better than you. It is best to specialise. If you know more about antique furniture than porcelain, then concentrate on that field. Some people specialise in house clearances, for people whose relatives have died or have gone into a nursing home.

Costs

Time and money are all-important costs. You definitely need quite a lot of money at first to build up your stock. Either that or you need to be commissioned by friends and dealers to seek out particular items for sale.

Time is perhaps the biggest cost. You need time to buy and sell items. You have to set aside time to scan market stalls, antiques fairs and antiques shops for bargains. This may mean driving to small country towns to find stock to sell. You also have to attend auctions and bid for items.

Then you need to decide how you will sell your antiques. Again this could be at auction, at antiques fairs or you could open an antiques shop (in the right area) or take a regular stall at a market. The most famous antiques markets in the UK are both in London: Bermondsey and Portobello Road.

How much can you make?

If (and this is a big IF), you know what you are doing, then you can make a fortune. If not ... So beware.

Where to find more information

The London and Provincial Antique Dealer's Association (LAPADA) represents people in fine art and antique dealers.

LAPADA
Suite 214
535 Kings Road
Chelsea
London SW10 0SZ
071-823 3511

The British Antique Dealers' Association (BADA) represents the interests of 400 members who have to adhere to the required standards of knowledge, degree of specialisation, integrity and quality of stock.

The British Antique Dealers' Association
20 Rutland Gate
Knightsbridge
London SW7 1BD
071-589 4128

ANTIQUES AND PICTURE RESTORATION

There has been a rapid rise in the value of antique furniture in recent years, and this has spawned a new industry of people setting themselves up as restorers. Picture restoring is a more traditional business, and for that you generally need to be qualified. Many of the courses on offer are post-graduate and are run by Courtauld Institute, the Hamilton Karr Institute at Cambridge University and the University of Northumbria. However, there are City and Guilds courses for those without degrees, and apprenticeships are still offered.

For more information and a booklet on careers contact:

The Conservation Unit
Museums and Galleries Commission
16 Queen Anne's Gate
London
SW1H 9AA
071-233 4200

The Association of British Picture Restorers also produces a guide to training. Write to:

Station Avenue
Kew
Surrey
TW9 3QA

Formal courses require a degree and individual training in a studio requires artistic ability and usually some scientific background.

Are you suitable?

You need good woodworking and materials skills for antiques restoration while to be a picture restorer you need artistic ability, manual dexterity, patience and perseverance. You need to gain experience with a qualified restorer.

Costs

For furniture restoration you need a large working area as well as storage space. Equipment, including specialist tools, will cost at least £2,000 but often more.

Equipping a studio for picture restoration is just as expensive, as you need an easel, a camera (to take photographs of details of a piece of work), and a binocular microscope. All this equipment could again set you back £2,000.

How much can you earn?

Everything is based on estimates and it depends whether you work for commercial art galleries or antiques dealers, museums, or private collectors.

Training

Courses in furniture restoration and picture restoration are held at the UK's premier arts and crafts college:

West Dean College:
West Dean
Chichester
West Sussex PO18 0QZ
0243 811301

But there is no substitute for on-the-job work experience.

Marketing

You have to find work by networking with antiques dealers, curators, and commercial art gallery owners. You will only get work from private individuals by recommendations and word of mouth.

Where to get more information

The British Antique Furniture Restorers' Association (BAFRA) represents the interests of its experienced furniture restorer members. You need to have been in business as a furniture restorer for at least four years to apply and be considered for membership of BAFRA.

British Antique Furniture Restorers' Association
c/o United Kingdom Institute for Conservation
6 Whitehorse Mews
Westminster Bridge Road
London SW1 7QD
071-620 3741

The Association of British Picture Restorers limits membership to those who can satisfy the governing Council that they are engaged full-time in the practice or study of picture restoration.

Association of British Picture Restorers
Station Avenue
Kew
Surrey TW9 3QA
081-948 5644

ANSWERING SERVICE

In the age of the answerphone, an answering service may seem redundant. However, as anyone who has an answerphone will know, many people do not like to leave messages. Or worse still, an urgent message can go unheard for hours, costing a business dearly.

Are you suitable?

To succeed as an answering service, you:

- Need a good phone voice and manner.
- Need to be well-organised.
- Must be reliable.

Cost

Fortunately, the cost of a telephone answering service is low as the phone calls are incoming for your clients and from them. They ring YOU regularly, say every half hour or hour to pick up their messages. You act as the office for them.

How much can you make?

If you have 10 business clients and they each pay you £50 a week, you could earn a total of £500.

Market research

You have to put a toe in the water and test the response to such a service in your area. It is busy one-man bands who need an answering service. Even though people have pagers and mobile phones these days, it is still impossible to get hold of them at times. Perhaps you could start with relations, friends, or friends of friends, to see whether or not it is feasible and workable.

Marketing

If you get over the first stage, then you need to advertise your services in shop fronts and in the local and regional press. Word of mouth and other recommendations would of course play a key part in building up your client base.

Pitfalls

An answering service is probably not viable on its own, and would probably be best as part of an overall secretarial and typing service. You could then get more income from each client.

Future

You could expand and broaden your clientele by offering more business services such as photocopying and faxing.

ART

If you are an artist—and this could be a latent talent or hobby, or one that you had before but gave up to concentrate on another profession—there are several things you can do to make money out of your talent.

You can paint and sell. You can set up a studio in your home and sell your works to local art shops, or if you are really good, to commercial art galleries.

Or you can paint portraits of tourists in the centre of the town or city you live in. You could start a handpainting service for local potters on a partwork basis. Finally, you could always give art tutorials to others.

Are you suitable?

You need talent, that's the most important requisite.

Cost

Just materials, which if you include all the paper, canvas, paints and an easel, can be quite expensive.

How much can you make?

As an art teacher you can earn from £15 an hour upwards for an art tutorial session. As for painting itself, it depends on market forces and others' perception of your talent and your work.

Qualifications and training

Not essential unless you want brush-up on your skills. You can go to evening classes and part-time classes at local colleges of further education or art schools.

Where to get more information

Try your local art school or college of further education.

AUCTIONS

Auctions are ideal hunting grounds for those who have—or are planning to—set up a retailing business such as a market stall or even a catalogue shopping service. Check out your local phone book for auction houses. Some specialise in selling computers, cars or bankrupt stock.

Lost and found auctions

Lost and found auctions are also worth a visit. The police and British Rail both auction off recovered goods. Always check out other dealers at an auction so that you are not trying to outbid professionals, and try to pick an area without much competition. So if everyone is buying up furniture, why not specialise in lamps and lightfittings or mirrors and prints.

Are you suitable?

You need money and an outlet for the goods you buy—ie a market stall or advertising in the press.

Costs

Transport (needed when buying in bulk), storage space, and money (again).

How much can you earn?

As items are bought at reasonable prices, your mark-ups (particularly for original, next-to-new, or antique items) can be 100 or even 200 per cent without pricing yourself out of the market.

Marketing

If you don't sell your stock through the newspapers or on a market stall, then you need to establish good contacts in the wholesale or retail market you are involved in.

Bankrupt stock auctions

This may seem as though you are preying like a vulture on the victims of recession. However, if you don't someone else will.

How do you make money? When a firm or household goes into bankruptcy, a receiver is appointed to sell off any assets to repay debts. However, bankrupt stock tends to be sold at fairly low prices.

You will generally find out about auctions and sales through the *Financial Times*, and local and regional daily and weekly newspapers.

Are you suitable?

You have to have enough spare cash to speculate and confidence in the items you are going to sell on.

Costs

A 'war chest' or kitty to buy items at auction, and the cost of storage.

How much can you make?

You can make a fortune or nothing. It is that risky a venture. If you are lucky, know your market, and find a market for the items that you want to sell on, then you can do extremely well. If you don't, then you could be left with a hole in your pocket.

Marketing and marketing research

See what the demand in your area is for certain items. If your local auction house deals primarily in secondhand furniture and the local market has a lot of people selling computers or records, then stay well clear of those items. You may prefer to deal in ornaments — something totally different.

Do your research, attend a couple of auctions, and test market the goods by buying a viable minimum amount.

To sell your stock you can either take a shop, advertise in newspapers and magazines like *Exchange & Mart* (or in the specialist magazines for the items you have bought) or sell them on a market stall.

So, for instance, if you bought up 40 items for £5 each, you would have spent £200. You would have enough stock to have a stall for a day at a market, where you would need to sell say 12 items for the same £200. If the stall costs £40 for the day, including transport, that would cover costs. You would still have 28 items to sell for your profit. But remember, it is best (but not essential) to sell stock that you have some knowledge about and where competition is not severe.

The market for office furniture and computers is fairly sewn up. But you can speculate and specialise in smaller consumables. While there are numerous dealers all round the UK buying up cookers, sofas and other popular household items, you could instead specialise in lamps and lampshades — the sort of things people would buy secondhand, unlike towels or beds.

Or you could buy a certain type of product at auction and give it added value. Curtains are a case in point. If you are a dab hand at sewing and making curtains, then you could buy bankrupt stock of materials from a local fabric shop that has gone bust and make curtains out of the material and sell them on.

Alternatively you could attend auctions of household contents to buy curtains which could then be altered and resold.

Pitfalls

When you go along to an auction, thoroughly inspect the stock in advance of the auction proper before bidding — otherwise you could, for instance, end up with the shell of a computer with all the essential components removed. Take an expert friend along if you are in doubt or are not familiar with the goods you intend to bid for.

BABYSITTING

Most babysitters are either part of a babysitting circle, friends who have their own children, grandparents or young teenagers looking to earn some additional pocket money (and it is also a good environment for doing extra studying).

Even so, if you have children or know people with children, you probably know how difficult it is to get babysitters and often parents are housebound as a result.

So you could make a bona fide business out of it. You can also combine this work with other work at home — anything from typing to ironing. Remember there is nothing to stop you making money while you are making money.

Are you suitable?

If you like children or have children of your own then you could consider it. You need to be trustworthy and responsible. Parents need to be sure that they can trust you with their offspring.

Costs

Just a telephone and time.

How much can you make?

Rates start at about £2.50 an hour. But if you actually start a babysitting network and you gain a reputation for yourself (and your network of staff if you expand), then depending on the area, you can probably more than double that.

If you decide to 'work' other areas, start with your friends in those areas where there are a lot of couples who need your type of service.

Market research

Check out the area. Make sure the local area you intend to work in has a lot of professional working couples who would like to go out regularly. It is very much a demand-and-supply type of occupation. You also need to find out if the area has strong babysitting circles already. Test-market your idea by starting with your local friends.

Marketing

Start with personal recommendations, then with cards in local shops and newsagents, and as you grow, take out notices and advertisements in the local press. Personal recommendations will be the best method, so tap into your network of friends.

Pitfalls

The only pitfalls are difficult children, demanding parents, and any crisis that occurs while you or your staff are on babysitting duties.

BEAUTICIAN, BEAUTY THERAPIST, ELECTROLYSIST

This is a great job if you are into looking good and looking after yourself. It particularly suits women. It is a very versatile type of profession that can be fitted into any daily timetable. You can travel to a client's house, or set up a room in your own home to carry out treatments on clients.

In this field you can either become a qualified beautician (which covers skin care, facial treatments, manicure, and so on), a qualified beauty therapist (which encompasses body massage, toning and slimming treatments, exercise, heat treatment and skin anatomy and physiology), or a qualified electrolysist (who specialises in the methods for permanent removal of unwanted hair). It is best to get qualifications to gain credibility — although they are not essential. If you are a good manicurist, for instance, you could probably build a reputation quite quickly among your friends and even set up in a corner of a local hairdressing salon.

How much can you make?

It depends what you do: you can be self-employed and build up a clientele by working from your own home, your own shop or taking space at a hairdressing salon; you can work for a cosmetics company as a consultant; or you can freelance as a make-up artist in television and theatre. However you work, you can charge a minimum of £15 an hour.

BADGE-A-MINIT

Badge-A-Minit opens up a world of opportunities to you with badges! If you are like most people, you probably would like to have a little extra money in your pocket. But how do you get that extra cash without investing high dollars first in a product or franchise? And what is your guarantee that people will buy your product or service? Badge-A-Minit is your guarantee because it's easy and inexpensive to make money with badges!

Everyone loves badges. They are perfect for so many events, activities, occasions or just for fun! Badges can be used to promote, advertise, inspire, communicate or motivate. With all these uses, selling badges is easy and profitable.

Most people would be surprised if they knew how much profit could be made on a single badge. Badge profits range from 100% to over 300% on average! Badge-A-Minit sells badge parts in quantities beginning with 50 parts at about 14p per badge – and going as low as 7p per badge in higher quantities.

Finished badges typically sell for £1 or more. Photo badges and one-of-a-kind personalized badges can sell for £2.50 or more. So it's possible to make anywhere from 50p and up on a single badge that takes less than a minute to make. And with a Badge-A-Minit badge-making system, you can easily make 50-300 badges per hour!

Badge-A-Minit offers several badge-making systems starting at only £19.95. All of the badge-making systems are designed to make professional-quality 57mm (2¼") pinback badges like the ones sold in gift shops.

Your badge-making system is an investment that will be sure to gain you a profitable business. That's why every Badge-A-Minit badge-making system has a LIFETIME GUARANTEE:

> "If any part of your system should, under normal operation, break or fail to function, we will repair or replace the part free of charge for the lifetime of the machine."

There are so many ways to sell your badges...

● Set up a booth and sell badges at shopping centres, flea markets, or fairs
● Arrange with local stores to display your badges near the cash registers.
● Take orders for personalized holiday or special occasion badges, refrigerator magnets or key chains.
● Get an instamatic camera and sell photo badges. These can sell for £2.50 or more!
● Call on fraternal or civic groups for I.D. badges, fund raisers or event promotions.

Getting started with your very own badge business is easy. Just see the Badge-A-Minit advertisement on the adjacent page to order your Starter Kit today or send for a FREE catalogue which features all the badge-making systems, parts, accessories and a full-line of stock badge designs.

With Badge-A-Minit, you can start your own badge-making business and watch your profits go up and up!

Qualifications

There are four courses you can take in the beautician/therapy field that can give you a qualification: Beautician Diploma Course, Body Therapist Diploma Course, Electrolysist Diploma Course and Assistant Beautician Certificate Course. Courses usually take between six months and a year to complete. Few grants are available for beauty therapy courses. They are run at various colleges round the UK. You have to be at least 17½ years old to take an examination and have three 'O' levels.

If you want to work in television, the BBC for instance requires candidates to be at least 21 years old, and to have two 'A' levels. All other commercial network TV companies require you to be at least 21 years of age, to have '0' levels and to be a fully qualified beauty therapist/hairdresser. You first need to gain some experience through an amateur dramatic group, working as a make-up artist.

Where to find more information

The British Association of Beauty Therapy and Cosmetology is one of the main trade bodies for this profession. It advises on training and qualifications and one of the main benefits of membership is the third party insurance scheme it has against accidents from negligence in connection with the treatments.

British Association of Beauty Therapy and Cosmetology
Parabola House
Parabola Road
Cheltenham
Glos GL50 3AH
0242 570284

Are you suitable?

You need to have a pleasant, sympathetic personality and the ability to deal tactfully with all types of people. You also need to look good yourself. But that doesn't mean you have to look like Michelle Pfieffer, just well-groomed, stylish and healthy looking. Inevitably treatments include close contact between a therapist and client. Can you bear treating skin allergies or dealing tactfully with clients who are not that hygienic?

Costs

The main cost could be training and gaining qualifications, up to £2,000 for a six month course. After that the equipment you need to use: state-of-the-art equipment for heat treatments, skin tanning, electrical treatments for slimming and toning and electrolysis can be very expensive; thousands of pounds in some cases.

BULK BUYING AND SELLING

Most retail businesses — even the local corner shop — buy large amounts of stock at wholesale prices, and sell the same stock in smaller batches with mark-ups.

To start a wholesale bulk buying and selling business you need to work out what all your costs are. You have to cover the cost of starting up — and particularly the initial investment in stock — staff costs (if you have any), premises and storage.

So, although you won't become a Tesco or B&Q overnight, you too can make a mark-up on items if:

- You know where to get goods at a reasonable price.
- You have a ready market.

For example, if you are a keen gardener and your friends are as well, why not bulk buy bulbs, fertilizer, and other items at a discount from a wholesale garden supplier or nursery or market garden, and sell these on to them? You would get the products you personally need for your garden at a cheaper price and you could undercut local gardening stores and make a profit — provided you do not get overextended and only buy items you know you will sell. But remember you will be up against strong competition.

Make sure you deal in a product that people have to restock on a regular basis — it will obviously be easier to sell than an item bought once or twice in a lifetime (unless you sell it at a substantial discount).

Are you suitable?

You need to deal in something you know quite a lot about, don't meddle in goods you don't. And you need to be confident that you can 'shift' enough goods to make a living.

Costs

Whatever type of goods you decide to sell, you will need to invest in stock and perhaps tie up a lot of money. And if these are perishable items like some plants or foodstuffs then they might have to be:

- Sold on quickly.
- Kept under certain storage conditions — refrigerators, a cold room, greenhouses, etc (and the costs that are associated with expensive equipment).

You will also need to have a van to carry goods around — from the wholesale outlet and to customers.

How much can you make?

If the competition is not stiff and you are able to undercut whatever little competition exists, then you could make a very good living out of bulk buying and selling.

Market research

You are selling wholesale and in bulk, so your main competition by and large will be retailers — whatever you sell. Survey the area you intend to serve. Are there already a lot of shops for the goods you intend to sell? If so, how good are they and what are their prices like for the basic products you intend to bulk buy? If all the signs are good, then you start your business. Also research wholesale distributors and see if you can buy direct from the manufacturer and check out their credit terms.

Marketing

You have to provide a prompt service and make it difficult for your customers even to consider going to a shop for the goods you will be selling them at reduced prices. You can order according to demand and offer a prompt home delivery service, but at a cost that covers transportation.

At first you will rely on the enthusiasm and support of friends who have agreed to buy your goods. After that you will depend on them 'spreading the word'.

You could always advertise in the local press, *Exchange & Mart* and organise a leaflet drop to drum up new business. Local newspapers might well be intrigued by your enterprise and feature you in an article.

Pitfalls

You may have to spend a lot of money buying stock, and for this you will need finance, which can make the operation very expensive.

You always run the risk that you will not be able to find buyers for your stock at a good margin.

Try always to be wary of selling stock for which you are not paid. Aim for cash in hand sales at the beginning and then carry out credit checks on your customers before allowing them to pay by cheque.

If you build up a good reputation you may get credit terms from the wholesaler or manufacturer giving you so many days, weeks, or months to pay. If you get cash from your customers before this time, you will then get money in before paying any out.

CAR BOOT SALES

Car boot sales are the phenomenon of the austere 1990s. Throughout the UK, people with little money or wanting to increase their income have discovered that junk and unwanted goods — from old irons to children's clothes — sell, and there are thousands of people out there willing to buy them.

But now, from being a simple extension of a jumble sale in the open air, car boot sales have become big business for organisers and new outlets for wholesalers (and dodgy dealers). At the large car boot sales, people who have bought bankrupt stock or goods at wholesale set up dedicated stands that sell the sort of wares you would find in any high street or market stall — household goods, car parts and accessories, hardware items, and garden equipment.

One way to make money is to hold or help organise car boot sales, rather than going along to them. Or to scour them for items of value (along with hundreds of others!).

Are you suitable?

You need to specialise in something that you know will sell at a large car boot sale, or invest in a lot of stock (much of it could be bought at previous car boot sales) to entice customers. You also need to enjoy bargaining with customers, getting up early on a Sunday morning, and driving quite a long way to a good car boot sale.

Costs

All the stock you can afford to buy.

How much can you make?

It all depends on how successful you are. If you earn £150 or more per car boot sale (less the site fee) then you are doing pretty well. It is worth continuing and persevering. However, be warned, many people do not cover their costs let alone make a profit.

Market research

The *Sun* newspaper publishes a weekly guide to all the car boot sales in the UK. Check out the ones within driving distance of your home. Find out the names of the organisers. Some organisers run successful car boot sales every week at the same site, while others rove from site to site, much like a circus does. Follow the most successful ones, the ones that promote the event well and get lots of sellers and buyers to attend. Also take note of the sorts of items that sell and don't sell.

Finally, location is all important. Is it easily accessible? Is it near a large urban area? Is it in a rich area or a poor impoverished area. If the answers to these questions are favourable, then you could do well.

Pitfalls

You could spend £10 to £15 on a site (or position) at a car boot sale and only make £10 in sales. If you did that too regularly you could be in the red before long.

Future

If you are successful at car boot sales, and want to work a stall full time, and not just as a way of making a relatively small amount of extra income, then you could upgrade to a market stall in a general street market or a specialist craft or antiques market. But you must develop a specialisation.

CAR BUYING AND SELLING

It's amazing how many people are in the second-hand car buying and selling business — even Arthur Daley from Minder. However, there is a lot of competition.

The alternative to buying and selling cars is setting up a car parts business. For this you need to go to breakers' yards and to select and buy car parts — anything from steering wheels to back axles.

If you specialise in car parts for an unusual or vintage car you could carve out a particular niche in this market and do particularly well. They are much in demand because they are very rare, and highly expensive to reproduce in custom form. Remember the old adage 'The sum of the parts is greater than the whole'.

Are you suitable?

To be a car buyer and seller, you need a wheeler-dealer mentality, and you need to know a good car from a duff car. You also need to go to car auctions to pick up some of the best bargains and be first to make a bid for cars in *Exchange & Mart* and the local press.

If you prefer to concentrate on supplying car parts you need to love cars and be a walking encyclopedia on cars and their parts. You also have to be prepared to muck in and walk round the dirtiest, oiliest scrapyards around to find what you want.

Costs

Buying and selling cars is an expensive business, so you need to rent a very good on-road site, and to have thousands of pounds available to buy cars.

With car parts the story is much the same, although you may only need a small warehouse unit or workshop, and the costs of parts. However, it is a cash business, so you won't have the problem of long-standing debts.

How much can you make?

If you have a good site then you could make a lot of money in second-hand cars — but the recession has hit a lot of businesses.

When dealing in car parts it is very much who you know. You need get a good reputation as a supplier for vintage car dealers and enthusiasts.

Market research

This only affects car buyers and sellers. You have to know how much competition you will be up against in an area, unless you specialise in, for example, American cars or vintage cars.

Marketing

Car buying and selling is essentially a commodity business. To make money you need a high turnover. So you have to have bold signs outside your forecourt area that demand to be seen. You also need to advertise heavily in the local press or specialist car press to get this high turnover.

Car parts selling is totally different. You need to find markets for your parts. You are only interested in enthusiasts and car dealers that specialise in the car parts you intend to supply. You will need to advertise in the specialist car press, but you will also need to make contact with car clubs — eg the MG Owners Club.

CAR CLEANING AND VALETING

Car cleaning and valeting has been a boom business in recent times. It can still be one of the most profitable sole-trader jobs to be in.

In the last five years a new, sometimes irritating phenomenon — possibly a sign of the recession — has surfaced: kids washing car windscreens at traffic lights. But even though their services are waved aside quite often, at 50p or £1 a time even they are making money.

Car cleaning is often run as a franchise — some of the big operations are — even though it has its origins in the boy scouts, who would clean your car for 'a bob'.

Are you suitable?

You don't need many skills for this job. However, you do need to be professional, and be prepared to work hard and fast.

Costs

How much a car valeting and cleaning service will cost depends on the type of service you offer. If you decide to run a mobile valeting service, then you will need a clean-looking mini-van, a handy vacuum cleaner and generator, a good water tank and hose, as well as all the cleaning and waxing materials necessary. You need to look the part and be truly professional.

But, if you intend to run a car valeting service on site, you will probably need a workshop with plenty of space and a forecourt, preferably one near a main road, as well as all the necessary cleaning and washing materials and equipment. If you buy a franchise this could set you back thousands of pounds.

How much can you make?

You can make a lot of money if you promote your services well, and provide a fast, professional service. There is even more to be made if you can negotiate exclusive contracts with car hire firms, car dealers, taxi companies and fleet managers in large companies.

You could specialise in one make of car for car dealers. Second-hand car dealers need to have their cars cleaned (and a full valeting service) before selling them, and particularly for top-of-the-range executive and sports cars.

Market research

Check out the local competition. Remember, to some extent, you would be competing with the automated car wash services at petrol stations. But many motorists shy away from them because they often damage their paintwork and windscreen wipers.

Marketing

You should consider advertising in the local press, and in the *Yellow Pages* and Thomson's local directories. You could also try and put cards in local car accessory shops.

When it comes to getting volume contracts you should speak or write to taxi firms, fleet managers, car dealers, and car hire firms.

The most important thing you can do is ensure that you give a very satisfactory service because repeat business is without doubt the cornerstone of success in car cleaning and valeting.

CAR REPAIRS

If you already have a number of years under your belt working for a car repair firm, or if repairing cars is your main hobby, you could do worse than set yourself up as a sole trader repairing cars. There is always a demand for good mechanics.

Are you suitable?

You not only need an interest in cars, and experience of repairing cars, you also need to want to repair cars day in and day out.

An Exciting Opportunity – Printing From Home

To be able to gain the benefits of 30 years experience of a proven and successful business is always a tremendous advantage – and for those who acquire the **'Blockmaster' Business Opportunity**, it will be the entry into an exciting new money making profession.

The 'Blockmaster' Opportunity is a unique Home-Based operation, which can be developed either as a part time or full time business with genuine potential to grow into a full time business with minimal capital outlay and little financial risk.

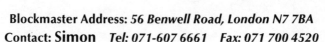

The 'Blockmaster' business, which reaches more than 60 countries worldwide, is a household name in the foil printing industry.

Blockmaster machines are extremely versatile and easy to operate. Several colours can be printed simultaneously, giving endless potential for personalised gifts, souvenirs and promotional items. The machines are capable of producing over 1500 impressions per hour.

Blockmaster also provides a full back-up service supplying foil, dies and 'printables'. A 24-hour block-making service and artwork facilities are available together with a life-time advisory and after sales service.

Blockmaster hotfoil blocking machines leave their mark on a wide range of products and materials such as paper, board, plastics, leather, wood, satin ribbon amongst many other surfaces.

For many people this will be the move towards a totally independent, lucrative and exciting new future, **buying direct from UK's longest established table-top machine manufacturers.**

Blockmaster Address: 56 Benwell Road, London N7 7BA
Contact: Simon   Tel: 071-607 6661   Fax: 071 700 4520

Costs

You need to rent a cheap workshop or small industrial unit to carry out the works. You will also need a wide range of tools which could cost hundreds of pounds — unless you buy them secondhand.

How much can you make?

Many car mechanics specialise in particular makes of cars or vans — a foreign make like Citroen for instance — so that they get a reputation amongst individuals and fleet car organisations, and by implication get more business that way. But that may not be an immediate option.

Self-employed mechanics or small car repair shops typically earn £15-20 plus an hour. Give estimates not quotes — quotes tie you down too much, and a job may turn out to be more complicated than it appeared on first viewing.

Qualifications

If your knowledge is a bit rusty, or you have gaps in your car repairing experience, then you could take a BTEC or a City and Guilds course and examination on car repairs before starting your business.

Market research

Simply see how many car repair shops there are in your area. Then you will know the sort of competition you'll be up against.

Marketing

Be sure that you offer a good service. If people are either dissatisfied with what you do, or they don't feel you are giving them value for money, then bang goes your reputation.

Advertise in the local press, in local shops and by leafleting house-holders. Word of mouth will be your best advertisement though.

CATERING AND COOKING

This is one of the easiest areas to make extra money if you already have an interest and a talent. You can start working from home and, if you only cook to order, can keep the risks to a minimum. However, there are strict Health & Safety requirements to be met and there tends to be tough competition.

Qualifications

If you want really want to be the best then you should either go to technical college to take a course in catering or in your chosen field (such as cake icing and decoration).

If you have the money though you could travel up to London to train as a chef at Leith's School of Food and Wine for certificate and diploma courses — fees currently start at £2,500 and rise to £7,200 depending on the course. An alternative is Le Cordon Bleu where the courses are more specialist and are less expensive — around £2,800. But there are also evening courses.

Leith's School of Food and Wine
21 St. Alban's Grove
London W8 5BP
071-229 0177

Le Cordon Bleu
114 Marylebone Lane
London W1M 6HH
071-935 3503

Are you suitable?

You will need to be prepared to work hard and often long hours to meet urgent orders. And you must be a good planner. It also helps if you enjoy what you are doing. And you will also need a good sized kitchen that meets food regulations that you do not mind dedicating to your business. Separate food storage for your professional cooking and catering will be required.

Costs

Keeping within the law will be a major expense. Food must be stored at the correct temperature. The Food Safety Act 1990 makes it an offence for anyone to sell or process for sale food that is:

- Harmful to health.
- Contaminated to such an extent that it would be unreasonable to expect it to be eaten.
- Falsely described, advertised or presented.
- Not what the customer can reasonably expect.

The law also requires that you must register a food business with the Local Authority Environmental Health Department. Registration is free and their regulations cover hygiene and safe premises. Get further advice from your local Environmental Health Department.

The Ministry of Agriculture, Fisheries and Food also runs a consumer helpline. Tel: 071-238 6550. MAFF produces a guide to starting and developing a small food business, this details the regulations and requirements that you must meet. A guide to the Food Safety Act is also available from:

Food Sense
London
SE99 7TT

You will also need to have enough cashflow to buy ingredients and pay for staff and advertising before you get paid for your goods or services.

Marketing

If you are good at cooking, you must then decide what type of catering business you want to set up. Here are some ideas for products or services you can make or offer from home:

● Jams and preserves
● Pickles
● Patés
● Catering for local business lunches
● Wedding, party and banquet catering
● Cake baking and decoration
● Pastries
● Biscuits
● Home-made ice cream
● Ready-made frozen dinners

For those with more cash and who are more ambitious, there is the option of setting up your own restaurant, cafe, winebar or take-away service. But remember the costs can be high, and with tough competition it can be easy to fail. A food franchise may be a safer bet for those wanting to set up their own food outlet.

The opportunities to sell your wares are almost unlimited. Consider the following:

- Offer nicely presented and unusual foods for sale through a local delicatessen and give them a cut.
- Check out local farm shops, craft fairs and markets to see if you can get a stall selling your beautifully packaged jams, preserves or pickles.
- Advertise your cakes in local papers and wedding magazines.
- Contact local businesses to see if they need someone to come in and provide a catering service for special occasions or business functions.
- Contact local pubs to see if they want someone to offer ready-cooked lunches or nicely prepared sandwiches.
- Ask local function rooms if they offer a catering service, and, if not, if you can work with them.
- Make the most of friends and existing contacts. When someone has a party or function offer to provide the food.

It is essential that your food is well presented. Make a virtue of the fact that it is home made with hand-written labels or carefully arranged displays.

How much can you make?

This depends on how big a business you want to set up. Always check out the competition. For instance, if your local delicatessen sells freshly baked patisseries find out how much they buy them for, and offer them a bigger margin for selling your product. But always remember, you must price your products or services to make a profit as well as to be competitive enough to sell.

Pitfalls

If you fail to plan, price, and market your business effectively, you could be left with masses of unsold stock. As a result it is best to take a deposit for large orders to help with cashflow and protect you against late, or non, payment.

Future

Again this is up to you. You could end up selling your garlic strings or olive paté to Harrods!

Sandwich making and selling

This is an area that boomed in the 1980s when office workers did not have the time to go out and buy lunch or a sandwich. Instead they had their food delivered.

Sandwich making and selling is one of the growth areas in the fast food service industry. In London, for instance, there are some very successful chains of sandwich bars — such as the fast-growing upmarket sandwich parlour, Pret A Manger. From little acorns... But to start it is usually easier to offer a telephone service, rather than invest in expensive retail sites. Deliver copies of your menu or sandwich list to local firms and find out if someone already offers this service. If not, make up a basket of sandwiches and test market what you have to offer. Be flexible and offer to make sandwiches to order to cater for unusual tastes.

CHILD CARE

Childminding

With more and more women wanting to or having to work, childminding is becoming an increasingly important service to the community in the UK. More parents choose childminding than any other form of daycare.

Up to two-thirds of mothers are in a job or looking for work and almost half have children under school age. But there are fewer than eight publicly-funded nursery places for every 1000 under-fives.

This creates good business opportunities for childminders, nannies and au pairs. Childminding is the most popular form of paid child care in Britain, catering for one in five youngsters in daycare.

Au pairs

While child-care services are regulated by the 1989 Children Act, anyone can become an au pair. No qualifications are needed. However, this is reflected in the level of pay. In exchange for accommodation and meals, au pairs get between £20 and £40 a week pocket money. Duties usually include a small amount of housework and childminding. Because it is a live-in job, it usually appeals to students and very young people.

Nanny

Nannies usually require more qualifications than other childminders. Many are trained as nurses or have gone on formal residential training schemes of which the most well known is the Norland Nannies scheme.

However, any reliable and presentable woman (few parents employ men) can become a nanny. Opportunities are advertised in magazines such as *The Lady*. Nannies are not registered and so parents may want to do their own checks on your background and will probably ask for references.

There are some 35,000 nannies in the UK. Wages average £183 a week for a nanny who does not live in and £131.22 for those who do. Most trained nannies have the NNEB (National Nursery Examination Board) qualification.

Are you suitable?

If you have children of your own and enjoy the company of children you could become a Registered Childminder. It is very rewarding.

As a self-employed day provider you have to be prepared to allow your home to be a den for children and the mess they create!

How much can you make?

You can charge between £40 and £100 per child per week as a child-minder, depending on the area you work in and the facilities you offer.

Regulations

If you want to start a childcare service in your home for children under the age of eight years, you must by law (Children Act 1989) be registered with the your local council's Social Services Department. You must also register if you look after children in your own home for more than two hours a day for reward or payment.

You can contact your local Social Services Office to get details of what regulations you need to adhere to, including home safety, health, fire and police checks. The Social Services can also provide training and support services when you start.

To be a Registered Childminder you have to pay an annual fee to your local council. As a Registered Childminder, you will be allowed to care for up to three children under five and a further three children between the ages of five and eight (including your own children).

You need to join the National Childminding Association and a local group to keep abreast of developments and advice and information.

Pitfalls

You could go ga-ga. You are with children all day!

Where to find more information

The main body that promotes the quality of childminding is the National Childminding Association. If you want to take childminding seriously then you need to join this association. It also produces useful publications such as the Childminder Handbook and Factfile and Childminding Contracts.

National Childminding Association
8 Masons Hill
Bromley
Kent BR2 9EY
081-464 6164

Playgroups and nurseries

This is the alternative to childminding. Pre-school playgroups and nurseries come in all shapes, sizes and types: family and drop-in centres, playgroups for children of homeless families, opportunity playgroups for children with special needs, playgroups for armed forces families, and parent and toddler playgroups. They are, however, for children aged between two and a half and five years.

They can be run by an individual with friends, or can be much larger groups run by a team of people in a public building, such as a church hall, community centre or another suitable premises.

Are you suitable?

Unlike a childminder, you need to obtain qualifications to run, or work for, a playgroup or nursery. It is more of a career and you need to be able to cope with large numbers of children. You need to be imaginative and creative with children.

Costs

If you decide to run a pre-school playgroup in your own home, you will need to spend some money. You will need to buy toys and games, drawing and painting equipment, and outdoor equipment such as a climbing frame, a sandpit, and swings.

You need to adhere to certain regulations. You will need to get planning permission from your local council to run a playgroup in your home, and register your playgroup with the local council's Department of Social Services.

You need to be familiar with the Children Act 1989, which relates to day care and education provision for young children (under eight years of age). You will also need insurance, and a Fire Office will have to inspect your premises to make sure they meet the required safety standards.

How much can you earn?

This depends on the size of your playgoup or nursery and how many children you look after. But you should be able to make a living, especially if you have a good sized home and turn some of it over to the business.

Qualifications

The recognised training for registered playgroup workers is the PPA Diploma in Playgroup Practice, which meets the criteria under the Children Act 1989. The course also provides students with the knowledge and understanding necessary for Levels II and III of the National Vocational Qualifications (NVQs) in Child Care and Education.

Where to find more information

The Pre-school Playgroups Association is the largest provider of pre-school care and education in England. It offers a range of training for those working in pre-school settings and fulfils the social services departments' requirements for registration. By becoming a member, you get and buy all the ready-made education tools and guidelines needed to start a successful playgroup.

The Pre-school Playgroups Association
61-63 Kings Cross Road
London WC1X 9LL
071-833 0991

Creche

Having got your childminding experience under your belt, and with your children now a little older and at school, why not approach large companies and organisations to see if they are interested in allowing you to set up a creche at their workplaces?

They are becoming more and more popular with so many mothers now working. And companies are becoming more willing to provide space for creches and even to subsidise the service and provide facilities.

Where to find your market

Contact the personnel manager or director of firms in your area to offer your services.

CHILDREN'S PARTY ENTERTAINER AND ORGANISER

You may not want to be the next Paul Daniels, but if you have a skill that appeals to children — acting, juggling, Punch and Judy, and magic — then there is a market out there for entertaining children at children's birthday parties. Following on from that, to ease the burden of host parents, you could also offer a full children's party service — organising all the activities, decorations, small presents and the food and drink, and clearing up the mess afterwards.

Are you suitable?

You need to like working for, and with, children (and not everyone can handle a room full of screaming and crying kids). The main thing is that you don't mind having jelly or anything else thrown at you. You also need to be able to deal with anxious mothers (if they attend) with tact and charm.

Costs

Buying all the equipment for your 'show' and, if you provide a full service, then all the presents, decorations and food and drink.

How much can you make?

You can charge anything from £200 upwards for a full children's party service. If you are the main entertainer, then you will need at least two helpers to look after the catering and keep control of the children.

Marketing

You need to advertise in the local and regional press, place notices in local shops, and cultivate your suppliers to recommend you whenever possible. Recommendations from satisfied parents will obviously be essential. You could also get repeat business. If Mrs A is satisfied with your services for Sammy's party to celebrate his third birthday, then she may ask you back the following year.

CLEANING

Commercial and contract cleaning

Service companies — which provide cleaning, building maintenance and building services, and catering — grew very fast in the 1980s as organisations contracted-out their core day-to-day running services.

Are you suitable?

To set up on your own you need experience of the cleaning industry, good administrative and negotiating skills, and some business to start you off.

Costs

At first you could start with a nice, liveried van, cleaning materials and, of course, ladders. Equipment is expensive, an industrial vacuum cleaner could set you back £200 or more for example.

How much can you make?

As long as you have negotiated a few contracts to start off with, you have a good bank manager and high ambitions, you could become the next Initial Services in time. In the meantime you have to be satisfied with small cleaning contracts for small businesses. Each one could work out at several thousand pounds a year.

Market research

Discover which cleaning firms operate in your area — local, regional and national firms — which businesses they work for, and find out how much they charge for their services.

Marketing

When starting your cleaning business you obviously need to place advertisements in the local and regional press, as well as sending mailshots to all the likely locations and office managers of the firms in your area. Attempt to get interviews with them to try to secure their business.

Future

If you build your business beyond the 'one man and his dog' level, and take on more staff and vans, then you need to advertise extensively in the trade press to bring in the larger contracts. These could net you about £500 a week each if they are for a large office or supermarket.

Where to find more information

The Cleaning and Support Services Association is made up of large and small companies whose core service is cleaning.

Cleaning and Support Services Association
Suite 73/74
The Hop Exchange
24 Southwark Street
London SE1 1TY
071-403 2747

Domestic cleaning

The 'domestic' is traditionally a very low-paid person who fits in cleaning someone else's house around bringing up children to boost their income or to fill their time during retirement. But as more and more couples work full-time, the demand for a cleaner is growing.

Are you suitable?

You need to be hardworking, multi-talented (polishing, ironing, cleaning, window cleaning can all be part of the job), trustworthy, and conscientious.

How much can you earn?

You can earn a fair wage if you manage to fill your days with daily morning and afternoon work. Wages vary from £3 to £5+ an hour. The best way to improve your prospects is through recommendations and word of mouth. If your employers are happy with your work, then they will recommend your services to other friends.

The other way to earn cash is to set up an agency. However, most householders like to know the person they are letting into their home and may not want to deal with an employment agency.

Total cleaning

What legacy do people leave when they move home or what confronts people when they move into a new home? Or what do you get when a house is left empty for a long period of time? The answer to all these questions is... mess!

A home needs a good springclean when this happens. It needs to be a quick in-and-out job, and professionally executed.

Are you suitable?

Have you any experience of cleaning and cleaning services? Do you have good contacts? And are you diligent, responsible and a good organiser? Then you could approach local estate agents to offer this as a service.

Costs

You cannot expect to carry out a fast and efficient 'total cleaning' service without staff — casual or part-time — who you can trust. You will also need to invest in a suitably sized van to carry all your cleaning materials, ladders, dust covers and so on.

How much can you make?

As long as you get regular work, you can negotiate very lucrative contracts. Remember individuals and businesses are paying for a thorough and fast service. You could charge at least £100 a day if the market can take it.

Marketing

Individual householders are one source of work, so you need to advertise your services in the local and regional press (as this total cleaning has to be a very mobile service you won't pick up that much work locally) and in the *Yellow Pages* and Thomson local directory.

But by far your most lucrative market will involve businesses, such as relocation firms and estate agents. In London, foreign embassies are also a good source of work. Staff are constantly on the move and renting apartments and houses that need 'total cleaning' before handing back to the owner or to another tenant.

(See Section on Commercial and Contract Cleaning for the Cleaning and Support Services Association).

Office equipment cleaning

Businesses usually employ cleaners and cleaning firms to clean every inch of their offices. But there are firms around which, strange as it may seem, offer one dedicated service: telephone cleaning.

But what about other sensitive telephonic and electronic office equipment, such as computer terminals, fax machines, photocopiers and mailing machines that all get filthy in the course of a week's use? They all need special treatment and a specialist knowledge of what methods and cleaning fluids can be used on them.

Are you suitable?

As long as you are not allergic to handling cleaning fluids and the fumes they emit, prepared to drum up custom, and ready to don presentable but practical work clothes, then you might make a good go of this.

Costs

Time, and the costs of the cleaning materials and fluids.

How much can you make?

You need to get business customers on contract, so the hardest job is negotiating a weekly or monthly fee for your services. And you need quite a few customers in a given area to make it pay. However, if you manage to get a contract with a large firm, they will have a lot of equipment to clean, so the work could be very lucrative indeed, particularly if you charge by the hour.

Marketing and market research

Approach local businesses and present your services to them. Try to convince them of the advantages of your approach — giving them a dedicated electronic and telephonic cleaning service. Ask them to give you a trial period, and if they are satisfied with your service, then they should be quite prepared to offer you a regular contract.

Brush up on your knowledge of cleaning methods by browsing round an office equipment shop or superstore, a DIY store, and by speaking to cleaning equipment wholesalers and manufacturers.

Write to the appropriate person — office manager, facilities manager, or managing director — at the firms you have found by thumbing through *Yellow Pages* and the Thomson local directory.

Future

This business has great growth potential, so you may get into a position where you can turn it from a one-man band operation into a small firm that serves a large area. And you could even diversify and establish a full office cleaning side to the business.

Carpet cleaning

Carpets are items that frequently need cleaning but require specialist equipment and an experienced person to operate it, although many offices and homes have three-in-one vacuum/cleaning machines. For a really thorough job more powerful equipment is usually needed.

Are you suitable?

You need to be prepared for hard work. Cleaning carpets is no doddle, and it can be very laborious. You also need to work unsociable hours — evenings, nights and weekends. It is a messy job and best done when there is no one about to keep disruption to a minimum.

Costs

The main costs are transportation (van or large car), chemicals and a steam carpet cleaning machine of the industrial type, which could cost you about £1,500.

How much can you make?

The work might not be too regular for each customer, but you should be able to get repeat business, particularly from the commercial sector. You could probably make about £10 or more an hour as a freelance contractor or £100 a day if you spend a few hours at each premises. Carpet and fabric cleaning tends to be charged out at a higher rate than normal commercial cleaning.

Marketing

To reach householders you need to leaflet your target area, advertise in the local press, and place notices in local shops.

When it comes to businesses, a mailshot to the possible premises and office managers should act as an introduction for an interview.

Pitfalls

During times of recession, carpet cleaning is deemed to be a non-essential, part of your job will be to persuade them otherwise. You will also need to insure yourself in case you damage a carpet or any soft furnishings.

COLLECTING

Why not turn your hobby into a job? It's been done before, and if you know your subject well, then why not? Collecting anything of worth can net you a small fortune if you know what you are doing. But you need to pick an area that can make money such as stamp or coin collecting, pop memorabilia, or rare books and records.

Are you suitable?

You will have an advantage if you own a good base collection to start with. You also need to know your subject well, and only pick a collectable that you do know something about. Perhaps coins are a better bet financially, but if you know nothing about them, then you could get your fingers burnt.

Costs

An established collection, money to invest, and knowledge.

How much can you make?

Luck plays a large part in how you fare as a collector because you often have to be in the right place at the right time to pick up bargains. But you can make your own luck by perseverance and by going out of your way to make good deals. You need to know your subject well, keep up with current values and sell at a good profit.

Market research

You have to do your research well including reading catalogues, magazines, collectors' manuals, and annuals.

Marketing

Attending fairs, and buying and selling collectables through dealers is the way that you will earn your living. You can advertise items for sale through the specialist magazines concerned with your subject area.

Pitfalls

Collecting is a risky business if you make it a full-time job. You can be 'stung' by conmen and sold fraudulant items. Also, the bottom can fall out of a market, leaving you with a loss on items you have bought. All markets recover in the long-term, but you might have to wait a fair while. So be careful.

COMMISSION-ONLY SELLING — PRODUCT DEMONSTRATION

You've seen product demonstrators and sales people at work in department stores showing you how a plastic kitchen gadget can save you time and effort. Or you've been approached by people at DIY stores offering you discounts on replacement (double-glazing) windows. They take a pitch and sell their products for commission only. If they don't sell anything, then they don't get paid.

Are you suitable?

You need to be thick-skinned (you're likely to be rebuffed frequently), pushy (in the nicest possible way), have gall, and be good humoured.

How much can you make?

Depending on the product line, the amount you sell, and on your commission rate, you could make a fairly good living. But you need to be prepared for little return during the first weeks. You have to gain experience and begin to understand the different types of people and what makes them buy. There is a very large drop-out rate due to the lack of success in this job.

INTERNAL REPORT

SELECT SERVICES
112 PORTNALL ROAD
MAIDA VALE
LONDON W9 3BG
(MOBILE) 0860 424344
(OFFICE) 081 968 4013

CONFIDENTIAL until now...

LATEST FIGURES – SELECT SERVICES MK1 (LONDON).
1993 (to date)

£ Turnover each month	% percentage increase (decrease)*
£2529.10 in January	(6.3%)
£2646.60 in February	(1.6%)
£3244.65 in March	+ 9.1%
£8420.35 1st Quarter '93	**+ 0.7%**
£2720.10 in April	+ 7.5%
£3073.10 in May	+ 16.1%
£3031.10 in June	(6.6%)
£8824.30 2nd Quarter '93	**+ 4.8%**
£3661.60 in July	+ 34.6%
£3395.60 in August	+ 10.5%
£3347.10 in September	+ 10.4%
£10,404.30 3rd Quarter '93	**+ 17.9%**
£3914.10 in October	+ 6.9%

COPY BANK STATEMENTS WILL BE SENT TO ALL APPLICANTS BEING CONSIDERED FOR SELECT SERVICES MK1

*: The Percentage Increase (Decrease) is analysed quarterly rather than monthly as most clients pay us by quarterly mandate. Each month is therefore compared with its counterpart three months before. The **quarterly** total figures show the gain (loss) on the previous quarter.

ANALYSIS

The agency has been expanding strongly throughout 1993. This is very promising. The third quarter of 1993 was our first to break into five figures – I see no reason why we should not remain above five figures from now on. (Demand for our service is so strong we couldn't stop our growth if we *wanted* to – except by unplugging phones!)

High rates of growth are being enjoyed by existing franchisees up and down the country, and there is no reason to suppose *new* franchisees will not find themselves kept similarly busy catering for the very high demand that exists in this lucrative service business.

ACCURACY OF FORMER GROWTH FORECASTS

On 10.08.93 I *forecast* our growth would stand at 10% for the last two quarters. (So far there has been 10.5% growth. August over May and 10.4% growth, September over June. The third quarter as a whole has shown a massive 17.9% growth over the second quarter.) I see no need to amend my earlier forecast for the moment, though it *may* prove to have been too cautious. We have not experienced this level of demand since the late Eighties.

FRANCHISEE GROWTH

Existing franchisees who are actively trading have now all reported in via a recent survey, so we know which areas need to be closed off. We still have a few empty areas which can accommodate more franchisees.

Any applications from people in areas where we have existing, *actively trading* 'Mk1' franchisees, will be sent details of our separate franchise business, 'MkII', instead.

This report (on Select Services London – the Mk1 franchise) is being circulated in 'The Daily Express Guide to Making Money' as a once only insertion. Applicants wishing to be considered for Select Services Mk1 are invited to complete the application form below. If the area you live in is already 'taken' by an active, trading franchisee, you may be invited to enter Select Services MkII. Note: MkII is a completely separate business.

NOTE: By the time you read this report, some time may have elapsed. We will therefore send all applicants full up to date figures for the intervening period.

For further details, send in the enclosed application form. We reply within seven days of receiving your form. Your details are kept strictly confidential and are not released to anyone.

- -

SELECT SERVICES APPLICATION FORM

NAME:
ADDRESS:
POSTCODE:
PROVIDE DETAILS OF PRESENT OCCUPATION:
PLEASE GIVE DETAILS OF OTHER BUSINESS ACTIVITIES:
EXISTING OFFICE FACILITIES – TYPEWRITER, COPIER, WORDPROCESSOR
DETAIL PREVIOUS BUSINESS EXPERIENCE (OR ATTACH C.V.)
SIGNED: DATED:
ADDITIONAL NOTES:
CODE: KP: DEG: 01 Select Services, 112 Portnall Road, London

CRAFTS AND ARTS

If you have an artistic bent, an existing talent, or even an interest in the crafts, then there are many opportunities to make a living.

Even the great and the good get involved in the crafts. Look at the way Princess Margaret's son David Linley has made a successful business out of cabinet- and furniture-making. Most people in the crafts are sole traders and more often than not, work from home.

Are you suitable?

Craftwork is ideal for someone with time on their hands and can be done in the evenings or combined with another job such as babysitting or telephone work. If you are unsure of the success of your venture, start small. Work part-time and sell to friends and colleagues to test the reaction to your work and your prices.

Qualifications and education

At any local technical college there are full-time, part-time and evening classes (some to Degree, HND, Diploma, and City and Guilds standard) in all types of craft and design.

The range of crafts is almost inexhaustible, but these are the main areas and there are courses in most of them:

- Calligraphy and lettering
- Candlemaking
- Carpentry, joinery and cabinet-making
- Crocheting
- Embroidery
- Enamelling
- Glass engraving
- Jewellery
- Knitting
- Lace making
- Lampshade making
- Leatherwork
- Metalworking
- Millinery (hatmaking)
- Model making
- Quilting
- Patchwork

- Pottery and ceramics
- Printmaking
- Rug making
- Sewing
- Silversmithing
- Stained glass making
- Stonemasonry
- Sculpture
- Textiles
- Upholstery and soft furnishings
- Weaving, spinning, and dying
- Wickerwork (basket making)
- Woodcarving

One of the main colleges for craft courses in England is the specialist West Dean College, which has short courses and workshops in most of the crafts in the list.

West Dean College
West Dean
Chichester
West Sussex
PO18 0QZ
0243 811301

Where to sell your wares

Try local gift shops, direct mail, or advertisements in newspapers, through your own catalogue, and at craft fairs or markets.

Market research

There is a growing demand for craft products. To be successful in this market though, you will need to conduct a good deal of market research to establish whether there is a market for your goods and what price the market can take.

Visit art and craft galleries and shops, markets, craft fairs and trade events. Read specialist magazines covering your subject area and read the 'small ads' and the larger display advertisements in these and in the local, regional, and national newspapers for ideas and prices.

Where to get finance

As well as the usual channels for finance mentioned in Part I, the Crafts Council has a 'Crafts Council Setting Up Scheme' (for England and Wales only), which is designed to assist selected craftspeople to set up their first workshop.

The Crafts Council scheme is for people who can show appropriate craft skills and originality of design. The Scheme consists of two parts, a maintenance grant of £2,500 for one year, and 50 per cent of the cost of purchasing or hiring equipment up to a maximum of £5,000. Scotland operates its own Start Up Grants Scheme.

Where to find more information

The Crafts Council is the largest of all the organisations devoted to the Crafts. It provides very useful information on setting up as a crafts worker, as well as all the ins and outs that that entails — tax, VAT, National Insurance, and Health and Safety. In addition, it publishes full details of all the courses run on crafts subjects throughout the UK.

The Crafts Council
44a Pentonville Road
Islington
London N1 9BY
071-278 7700

The Society of Designer Craftsmen acts as a point of contact for potential buyers wishing to commission works, organises get-togethers for craft members and organises exhibitions. The crafts practised by members includes: basketry, calligraphy, ceramics, furniture-making, glass engraving, jewellery, lettering, printmaking, sculpture, silversmithing, stained glass making, textiles, toymaking, and woodworking.

Society of Designer-Craftsmen
24 Rivington Street
London EC2A 3DU
071-739 3663

The Guild of Master Craftsmen represents the interests of members working in the crafts, particularly the self-employed.

The Guild of Master Craftsmen
166 High Street
Lewes
East Sussex BN7 1XU
0273 478449

Carpentry, joinery and cabinet-making

Even to consider becoming a carpenter and joiner, or specifically a cabinetmaker, you must have the talent and experience for this precise work. If it has been your hobby over the years, then, and only then, can you even begin to consider starting a business.

Are you suitable?

You need talent, skills, and often strength and stamina.

Costs

As well as a good-sized workshop, either at your home or a convenient site, other costs will include the very expensive tools and floor-mounted machinery that you will need to do a professional job.

How much can you make?

The very finest cabinetmaker can command thousands of pounds for highly designed and perfectly made furniture. A carpenter and joiner can charge fees that are sometimes higher than other crafts and trades associated with the building industry. As a carpenter you could be asked to make expensive sash windows to order (at about £250-300 a time), a new staircase (at no less than £750), or one-off doors or sets of room-dividers.

Market research

As a carpenter, you need to investigate what competition there is in the local area by thumbing through *Yellow Pages* and visiting the main ones to discover what sort of operations they are.

If you have the abilities necessary to be a cabinetmaker (a far more demanding and exacting job than carpentry and joinery) then you will have to cast your net further afield and attend furniture fairs, and independent furniture shops to gain ideas and gauge the competition.

Marketing

Carpenters and joiners usually advertise in local directories such as *Yellow Pages* and the Thomson local directory, so you would need to do the same. The local press is also a key source of new work if you place advertisements in their services sections.

Cabinetmakers need to get their works noticed by exhibiting at furniture fairs. You would also need to approach high-class furniture shops to encourage them to take your designer-furniture. You could also approach like-minded interior designers.

Embroidering

If you have a talent for this you could make gifts — such as embroidered napkins, pillowcases or handkerchiefs — and sell them through local craft shops or markets. Alternatively you could offer a made-to-measure service.

The Embroiderers Guild promotes all forms of embroidery and stitched textiles through teaching, study, and a variety of events.

Embroiderers Guild
Apartment 41A
Hampton Court Palace
East Molesey
Surrey
KT8 9AU
081-943 1229

Knitting

Knitting is a craft that many girls (and some boys) learn when they are very young from mothers passing on their skill. So knitting is something you can make good use of if you were taught at a young age and continue into later life.

Original woollen clothes, particularly sweaters, jumpers and cardigans, are very much in demand. How many times have you walked out of a high street store with a nicely designed sweater only see every Tom, Dick and Harry wearing the same?

Are you suitable?

You may be good at knitting, but can you imagine making a living from it full-time? And are you creative; can you come up with original designs? Or do you rely too heavily on patterns you buy in wool shops?

You will need to offer something special and different if you are to compete and make money from your knitting — whether it is clothes for babies or jumpers with silly patterns for adults.

Costs

The only real costs are your time, a large stock of different strengths and colour wools and a knitting machine to produce in volume.

How much can you make?

A strong, well-made woollen sweater with a striking and unique pattern can be sold for anything from £40. If you make a name for yourself in this market, then you can command well over £100 for your best sweaters as people will then be paying for the 'name'.

Marketing

You can be commissioned by individuals who will give you a brief of what they want and may take on board your design recommendations. Or you can sell your wares through local clothes shops, or by mail order through direct response advertising in newspapers and magazines.

Jewellery

Most markets have at least two stalls with handmade jewellery for sale — particularly earrings. Parts, beads, wiring and clips can be bought in bulk from wholesalers and made into your own designs.

Designer Jewellers Group
24 Rivington Street
London
EC2A 3DU
071-739 3663

Lace making

Lace is another popular item, particularly for those buying a gift. You can add lace to sweaters to make them special or even produce greetings cards with lace bows.

The Lace Guild promotes the craft of lacemaking, and offers membership to people with an interest in lacemaking — its history, origins and uses — including artists, craftsmen, and teachers.

The Lace Guild
The Hollies
53 Audnam
Stourbridge
West Midlands
DY8 4AE
0384 390739

Lampshade making

This is a very underrated craft. Most lampshades are mass produced, just like the lamps they are fixed on to. Original lampshades are few and far between, and interior designers are always on the look-out for original objects to fill a room.

You can study lampshade making at evening classes at local colleges.

Patchwork and quilting

This is another craft, ideal for someone with talent, patience and time on their hands. Again it requires minimum investment. You can make anything from patchwork quilts to quilted jackets.

The Quilters' Guild promotes every aspect of quilting and patchwork.

The Quilters' Guild
The Administrator
Dean Clough Business Park
Halifax
West Yorkshire
HX3 5AX
0422 347669

National Patchwork Association
PO Box 300
Hethersett
Norwich
Norfolk
NR9 3DB
0603 812259

Pottery and ceramics

If you want your work to be taken seriously so that it sells, pottery or ceramics must already be a hobby and pastime of yours. If not, you need to take a course at a local college or the West Dean College.

Are you suitable?

You need to be good with your hands and have a creative bent.

Costs

You need space. You could convert your garage, garden shed, or a workroom. In addition, you need the tools to do the job, and these don't come cheap (although you could buy them secondhand). You need a sink, a solid wooden worksurface, a damp cupboard, a waterproof container for storing clay, a potters wheel, and, of course, a large kiln. Then there are the smaller tools that you need to pot, such as sponges, brushes, modelling tools and cutting wire.

You also need to buy clay, which you can usually get from local brickworks, and the necessary materials to glaze the pots or ceramics you have made.

Marketing

Your main market for pottery and ceramics will be arts and crafts shops. The owners will either take your works on a sale or return basis, or buy a limited quantity and order more if they sell.

Alternatively, you could hire a stall at a general, or crafts, indoor or outdoor market and sell your work that way.

Where to find more information

The Craft Potters Association represents the interests of members involved in contemporary studio pottery. It is run by potters for potters, both professional and amateur, and for educationalists, collectors, and interested lay people.

The Craft Potters Association
7 Marshall Street
London W1V 1RD
071-437 7605

Sewing

Sewing is a wonderfully versatile skill to have. It bridges many areas such as dressmaking and clothes-making in general, as well as quilting and patchwork, and curtain making and soft furnishings.

But if you just concentrate on providing a repairs and alteration service, you could still be much in demand. What better service to offer busy people whose expensive clothes need altering due to weightloss or because of wear and tear?

Are you suitable?

You need patience, application, experience and a love of sewing.

Costs

Your main cost will be a first class electric sewing machine, which can cost a few hundred pounds.

How much can you earn?

If you build up a loyal local clientele then you could make a good living, particularly with all the repeat business you are likely to be offered. You could charge a competitive rate that slightly undercuts tailoring costs offered by dry cleaners.

You can also do part-work — making parts or all of your garments — for a fashion company. But the wages tend to be very low. Unless you are very good, very quick and can do your work while looking after children, it may not be viable.

Marketing

Word of mouth will be your most powerful sales tool. After that you can advertise your services in shop fronts, and in the local press.

CURTAINS AND LOOSE COVERS

Everyone needs curtains, but hardly anyone has the time or skills to make them. People can, of course, buy ready-made curtains, but although these are ok for bedrooms and bathrooms, they are not ideal for living rooms. So there is a market for good curtains and matching loose covers for sofas.

Are you suitable?

This is work only for the experienced sewer who has bags of patience. If you are, you can progress to curtain making by taking a course at evening classes at college to enhance your skills. You need to be a good brief taker, as customers are often a fickle lot. And you need to deliver on time. You mustn't take too many projects on at one time.

Costs

A very good sewing machine and a large spare room to work in so that you can spread your fabric around. Never buy the fabric yourself. But you could go round with the client and choose the type and amount that you need.

How much can you make?

If you start on your own, you can undercut the department stores and fabric shops. If you are making a set of curtains, your labour costs could be from £100 to £200, particularly if the work is intricate and you are asked to make curtains with swags and tails.

Marketing

You can advertise your services in the local press. You will also have to rely on word of mouth recommendations. If you do a great job, then the news will get round.

Future

If you do particularly well, you could either open your own fabric and curtains shop, or advertise your services nationally through the women's and home improvement consumer press.

CVs AND LETTER-WRITING

Many people are bad at setting out their CVs (Curriculum Vitae) and writing accompanying letters that have an impact on potential employers.

Equally, there are other occasions when business people and members of the general public need to write letters that have to be well-written and make sense. Finally, it could come down to logistics; some people just do not own a typewriter or personal computer and need a well-presented document prepared.

Are you suitable?

This is a great way for a copywriter or any person who has a good command of English to earn extra income. You also need to know about the layout of letters and how to write business letters.

Cost

Just time, if you already own an electronic typewriter or — even better — a personal computer or word processor with a high quality printer.

How much can you make?

Whatever the market can bear. But probably anything between £20 and £40 per CV would be a reasonable sum. For an executive CV you could charge £60. Or you would have to negotiate the fee in advance, based on the amount of work and time that you envisage you would spend, and stick to it rigidly.

You could also offer a target mail-out service whereby you send out CVs on behalf of applicants to companies that fit the applicants' job specifications and brief.

Market research

If you read the national quality press you should be able to see small advertisements quite regularly which promote these types of services. There won't be that many in your area.

Marketing

Advertise your service in the local press. The local paper may even write an editorial piece about what you do. Friends could recommend your services. You could also write to the heads of local schools and the student unions of local colleges with details of your service.

Future

If it takes off, then you could get a network of freelance colleagues to join you on a co-operative basis, and advertise in the national press.

DESKTOP PUBLISHING

Good, clear documentation with graphics is essential to some self-employed people and businesses. But they often can't afford to buy a desktop publishing (DTP) computer and software package, or they cannot justify having one on the grounds that it might only be used occasionally. Instead, they go to firms or specialists who can offer that service.

Are you suitable?

You need to be able to use computers and be knowledgeable and trained in the use of DTP. You need to enjoy working on your own, but at the same time dealing with people's needs. They often need work done 'yesterday' — in other words very quickly. So you need to be able to handle that pressure and work fast, and even into the night to complete a job.

Costs

DTP packages can be very expensive to buy. They start at £3,000 for a basic PC (personal computer), laser printer and software, although an £8,000 package is usually what is needed for a high turnover business. They can rise to £15,000 to £20,000 for a first rate DTP workstation and software to go with it. A top quality printer to give a professional look to your work is a must. For graphics and colour work, it may be cheaper to send disks to a printer than to invest in the equipment yourself.

How much can you make?

It all depends on how much custom you get. But the rates per hour can be very high for this specialist service, particularly if you can offer high quality graphics. You need to read the office trade press and computer press to see what the current rates are.

Qualifications and training

Formal qualifications are not necessary, but a thorough knowledge of your equipment is. A qualification in design or graphics will add extra credibility. Courses are available at some further education colleges, leading to qualifications, or private colleges run short intensive courses which can be good but rather expensive. Your local library or careers centre can advise you.

Market research

A trial advertisement or mailshot should be enough to see if there is a demand for your service.

Marketing

You can either set up your DTP service as a local service or widen the field to take in a bigger area. If you choose the local route, you need to mailshot or leaflet all the businesses in the area, and place advertisements in the local press. If you want business from elsewhere you can place small advertisements in the national or regional press, or the Office and Business trade press.

Future

If you get really well established then you could rent an office unit, take on staff, and offer other services — small printing and colour copying.

DESPATCH AND COURIER

The growth of despatch and courier services has been quite staggering in the last fifteen years, particularly in London.

Are you suitable?

You have to be a very experienced and exceptionally good driver or rider, and, if not, you should seek further training. You need a very reliable bike, motorbike or van, which should be in excellent working order. You should also like being at the wheel or riding for long stretches at a time and enjoy outdoor work.

Cost

If you are a van courier, then you might have to supply your own van (and possibly change the livery). If you are a despatch rider, then all you will need to buy is a bicycle or motorbike.

How much can you make?

A motorbike despatch rider can earn about £500 a week with a top despatch firm in London. A bike rider will earn quite a lot less because the distance that can be travelled is limited. A van courier driver can earn around £400 a week.

Where to get work

If you want to stay local then there should be courier firms reasonably near to where you live. If you want to earn more, then you will need to approach large firms in towns and cities. Their standards and requirements will be more stringent. You will have to prove your worth.

Pitfalls

Long hours in varying weather conditions. Riders and drivers are advised that they should not spend more than ten hours on a motorcycle or at the wheel of a van in any one day. Continuous riding or driving should not exceed four and a half hours. And a minimum of a half hour break must be taken at the end of this stretch of riding or driving. The accident rate among despatch riders is extremely high.

Where to find more information

The Despatch Association was formed in 1985 to improve the standards of the despatch and courier industry, and particularly the calibre of the riders and drivers.

The Despatch Association
5-11 Lavington Street
London SE1 0NZ
071-620 0775

DIRECT MAIL

Direct mail is a multi-faceted job. You have to know how to target markets, provide creative input for direct mailshots, organise mailings, and evaluate the results — that's if you provide a full service.

If you just concentrate on fulfilment; that is organising and sending out mailings — in their hundreds and thousands sometimes — then you are offering a service at the basic end.

Are you suitable?

This job is a slog at the beginning. You need to get first hand experience of stuffing envelopes by working for someone else. Then you can offer your services on a freelance basis, taking in mailshots to stuff into envelopes. Finally, you can set up business on your own.

Costs

There are no costs until you start working for yourself. Then you will need a mailstamping machine which can cost hundreds of pounds. You will also need a workshop with lots of space to store mailshots for distribution.

How much can you earn?

When working for someone else, you might only get as little as £2.25 an hour for stuffing envelopes, although a higher fee can be negotiated if you stuff so many envelopes per batch.

When you set up on your own, then you can earn much higher sums, which you negotiate with clients. By that stage you may be the boss hiring freelance staff on a piecemeal basis to work as and when you need them.

Market research

Check what the competition offers and read the trade press to check their prices.

Marketing

To get work for your business you need to approach local businesses and advertise your services in trade magazines such as *Direct Response* and *Precision Marketing*.

Where to find more information

The Direct Mail Association Services Standards Board is the body that polices the direct mail industry. To be a recognised member, you have to adhere to certain rules. Then you will be put on the DMASS's recognised list which is sent out to any enquirers.

The Direct Mail Services Standards Board
26 Eccleston Street
London SW1W 9PY
071-824 8651

DIY — ODD JOBBING AND REPAIRS

There is still a call for oddjob people, who can repair anything in the home — from an electrical appliance to shelves, from a crack in the wall to damaged skirting boards.

Are you suitable?

You need to have good all round DIY skills: to know a bit about this and a lot about that — 'A Jack of all Trades'. But for anything specialised — plumbing, electrical work, or gas installation — you need qualifications.

Costs

All you need is a good set of tools and materials to do all types of jobs. This could set you back a few hundred pounds or so.

How much can you earn?

You won't earn a fortune, but if you get a good reputation you could get very regular work. It might be best to offer your services in the evenings, at weekends, and on days off from your main job. Keep it as a useful second income job.

Market research

This is impossible to carry out. Just start your business in a small way and see if it builds up.

Marketing

The best way of getting your name around is by word of mouth and recommendation. Also put up notices in newsagents and other shops. Leaflet distribution could create some interest. It probably won't be worth your advertising in the local press unless you want to expand the business.

You want to be seen as reliable, cheap, and a good 'fixer' of people's DIY problems — it is amazing how useless some people are when it comes to assembling flat-packed furniture or even fixing a dripping tap.

DOG-WALKING

Many people have dogs, enjoy their company, but do not have enough time to exercise them properly. So this is where a good dog handler can play his or her part.

Are you suitable?

If you've time on your hands and own a dog of your own which needs regular walking anyway, why not exercise one or two more dogs at the same time? It would suit retired people or youngsters who need to increase their income or pocket money.

Costs

Nil.

How much can you make?

It all depends on the premium that owners put on the need to get their dogs exercised and kept healthy and fit. The income you could get would at least keep your own dog in doggy biscuits and pay for its veterinary bills or insurance — but you should be able to earn a good deal more.

Market research

Find out from dog-owning friends what they would be prepared to pay for a dog-walking service if they had to. And, do see before you start, that you can and want to be a dog-walker.

Marketing

If you don't have enough trade through your friends and relatives and initial word of mouth, then you could put an advertisement in your local paper or a dog owners' magazine (stating the area you live in). Also, place a card in your local corner shop or newsagent.

Pitfalls

If a dog in your care gets run over or badly hurt in a fight, you may have a lot of explaining to do.

Future

If you take to dog-walking, there is no reason why you should not turn it into a good small business, and employ others to carry out the dog-walking, with you taking a cut of the fee. You could also diversify into grooming if you are used to washing dogs and trimming their fur.

DOG TRAINING

Could you be another Barbara Woodehouse, the late, great TV dog trainer whom everyone knew for her catchphrase 'walkies'?

If you've always owned a dog, and you know a fair amount about the characteristics and behaviour of all the main breeds of dog, then you could always run a dog training school.

Are you suitable?

You need to be an experienced owner and have trained your own dog according to 'established' dog training criteria — and know all the commands.

Costs

The renting of a centre of some sorts — village or borough community centre, church hall or the like.

How much can you earn?

As a dog trainer or team leader, you could charge owners with their dogs £5 each for a group session. If you taught three or four groups, with ten dogs in each group containing dogs at different stages of learning, then you could earn between £150 or £200 a week. You could restrict teaching to evenings or weekends when both you and the owners would be available.

Market research

Obviously you need to find out if there are any other dog training schools in the area.

Marketing

Organise a leaflet drop to every home in the area, advertise in the local press, and ask friends and neighbours if they know of new dog owners. Also give details of your service to local pet shops.

DOOR-TO-DOOR SECURITY

There are too many frightened people around these days. Crime is on the up and homeowners need to take precautions to secure their homes and themselves far better than ever before.

They need above all to ensure that their first line of defence — their front door — is secure. They need spyholes and doorchains to stop unwelcome guests pushing their way through. So why not make the most of this? If you are handy, and have a battery operated drill and screwdriver, you can fit door chains, window locks and spyholes in a matter of minutes for cash.

Are you suitable?

You need gall and speed. You will need to be able to knock on any-one's door and sell your service quickly, and then carry out the job speedily. The service you offer can be one that doesn't require you to step beyond the front door mat by just fitting door security devices. Of course, you will need to be good at fitting devices (lock manufacturers may be able to help) and not look like a potential burglar.

Costs

The only costs for this job are a suitable neat uniform, and the tools to do the job — a battery operated drill, and a stock of spyholes and security door chains. These can be bought in bulk.

How much can you make?

You can probably charge as much as £10 to £15 (cash in hand) a house for parts and labour. If you do about 10 jobs a day then you are on for about £100 a day.

Market research

Contact lock manufacturers to find out bulk prices and if you need training. Survey a few streets in your area to find out how much demand there will be.

Marketing

You'll be surprised how few people have basic door security. They might have a yale lock or a chubb lock or both, but many do not have spyholes or doorchains.

Most of your work should come from knocking on people's doors, but you could supplement this by advertising in the local press, or by sending out leaflets the day before you call in the area — just to pave the way.

DRAIN UNBLOCKING

Drain unblocking is generally a mucky occupation that just needs a handyman to do — it doesn't require an experienced plumber.

Are you suitable?

You have to be prepared to work with muck, particularly if you extend your service to include toilet and sink unblocking. It's pretty disgusting work, but if you have a strong stomach, then why not?

Costs

Perhaps a van, and equipment: rods, suction pads and so on.

How much can you make?

Not as much as a plumber, but Dyno-Rod — very much a household name (and a franchise) — has created a profitable niche from unblocking drains. You can charge a call out charge of say £20 plus a fee on top for your time.

Marketing

You would have to start locally first, so your best way of advertising your service would be through local newspapers and notices in shops. You could also leaflet the area as well.

DRESSMAKING

If you are tall, short, chubby or an odd shape, then you will know how difficult it is to shop at C & A or Marks & Spencer (or even the 'in' fashion shops) for dresses and skirts that fit properly and suit your size and shape. Why not take advantage of this?

Are you suitable?

You need to be experienced in sewing and using sewing machines, and have an eye for dress design and choosing and recommending fabrics. If you concentrate on working from patterns and partworks, then the job is that much easier—you don't have to rely on your own designs—just on patterns bought from shops or catalogues. All you have to do then is buy the fabric and follow the pattern design instructions, cut it out and stitch it together.

Costs

An electric sewing machine is essential for dressmaking and this can cost several hundred pounds. Apart from that you need all the bits and pieces, such as zips, needles, thread, buttons and so on to make the dresses.

How much can you make?

If you are very good, then people will hear about you, and you will be able to produce a quality dress at a competitive price midway between the cheaper items found in shops and the more expensive ones. So if a cheap dress normally costs £50 in a shop and an expensive one £150 or more, then you could realistically charge about £80 for your labour.

Your success will depend on how fast you are and how much custom you can attract.

Offering a personal service can be popular, particularly if you involve your clients right through the process. It is important to have a fitting as soon as the garment is near completion, and a second one to check minor details at the end. Alterations can be time-consuming and fiddly, so this must be a cost that is built-in to your overall price.

Marketing

Obviously, recommendations will be crucial, but you can also sell your dressmaking skills through the local press and place notices in local fabric shops.

Should you decide to make off-the-peg items, then you could sell them through mail order in the small ads of women's magazines. But you must ensure that you have sufficient stock to fulfil orders.

Think about specialising — that way you will be able to build up a reputation more quickly. Wedding and bridesmaids' dresses are an obvious niche, as are clothes for children or the particularly small or large. A catalogue and a few samples are a good idea as your potential customers can see exactly how good you are.

DRIVING — INSTRUCTION

If you are a good, safe, and confident driver, and don't mind being at the wheel of a car for hours on end, you could find becoming a driving instructor a very rewarding job.

Costs

If you work for yourself then you will need to get a well-equipped dual-controlled car (small models are best), which could set you back £8,000 or more. It has to be in tip-top condition or else you could be struck off if Driving Standards Agency officials make an inspection and the car is found to be faulty. If you join BSM as a self-employed franchisee driving instructor, then you get a car supplied free.

You will probably also need an office to work from and a secretary to organise your bookings. Driving instructing is not a cheap business to run, there are many overheads.

How much can you earn?

Normal rates of pay start at £11 an hour up to about £19 at the top rate, depending on who you work for and where you work in the UK.

BSM drivers are franchised and therefore have to pay their first 16 hours a week to BSM. They work roughly 30 hours a week at about £16 an hour.

Qualifications

To qualify as a Department of Transport Approved Driving Instructor you need to meet certain requirements and pass three examinations. The requirements set by the Driving Standards Agency are that:

- You must hold a full British Driving Licence, and must have held a full Driving Licence for a minimum of 4 years prior to being accepted onto the register.
- You must have no criminal convictions unless they are spent.
- You must be able to read a car number plate at a distance of 27.5 metres, when the letter and numbers are 79.4mm tall.

The examinations are in three parts:

- Part One: is a written test of 100 multiple choice questions on general driving knowledge and the Highway Code.

- Part Two: tests your driving ability on various kinds of roads—urban, country and motorway.
- Part Three: is an instructional ability test which tests your ability to instruct.

Also, if you become a member of the Driving Instructors' Association, you can study for the DIA's Diploma in Driving Instruction.

Marketing

If you do not have the security and back-up of BSM, then you will need to advertise your services in the local press and *Yellow Pages.*

Where to find more information

The Motor Schools Association (MSA) sets standards of professional and ethical behaviour for its driving instructor members.

The Motor Schools Association
182A Heaton Moor Road
Stockport
Cheshire SK4 4DU
061-443 1611

The Driving Instructors' Association (DIA) represents 10,000 professional instructors in the UK. The DIA aids instructors with their businesses, and provides a whole range of services for instructors.

The Driving Instructors' Association
Safety House
Beddington Farm Road
Croydon CR0 4XZ
081-665 5151

The Driving Standards Agency (DSA), a government body, administers the Approved Driving Instructor Training Establishments Directorate (ADITE), which monitors and approves driving instructor training establishments throughout the UK and keeps an up-to-date list of ADIs. You can get a starter pack from the DSA for a nominal sum.

Driving Standards Agency
Stanley House
Talbot Street
Nottingham NG1 5GU
0602 474222

DRIVING — MINICABS

The market for minicabs (or private car hire) has grown tremendously in the last 15 years, particularly in London where the black cabs ignored their rise in popularity (and their customers' needs) until recently and lost business as a result.

Are you suitable?

You need to be tough and enjoy driving for hours on end. To get started it is best to try and get a job with a reputable local firm. It is then easier to get work. It can be a risky job, so be prepared for that. You will also need a clean driving licence, a four door saloon car and relevant insurance. You may also need to be licensed if you are based outside London.

Costs

You need a good, clean car. It should be a reasonable size; models like the Ford Sierra and Vauxhall Cavalier fit the bill. You needn't buy a brand new car, just one in good condition.

How much can you earn?

Minicab drivers can earn anything up to £450 a week if they are good and work for a firm that can give them lots of work.

DRIVING — CHAUFFEUR

Once you have been through the mill as a minicab driver you can move up a gear and become a VIPs' chauffeur.

Are you suitable?

You have to dress smartly, be courteous, and interested. Attention to detail is also important, as you have to keep your car clean at all times and offer your passenger every possible luxury and cater for every need—from car phones to daily newspapers.

Costs

Obviously it is best to work for a spell for a chauffeur company to gain experience. However, when you decide to go it alone, then you will need to invest in a top-of-the-range car such as a BMW, Mercedes, or Jaguar, and this could cost £25,000 plus. Insurance can be expensive when you run a driving business. However, you can buy this with a finance scheme and make repayments from your earnings.

How much can you earn?

A top freelance chauffeur is worth his weight in gold and so can earn a small fortune, particularly if you have excellent exclusive contracts with major businesses. It is not unheard of for a chauffeur to earn £50,000 plus a year. However, chauffeuring rates usually start at around £6.70 an hour.

DRIVING — FOOD HOME-DELIVERY

More and more restaurants and fast food outlets are opening and many want to offer a food delivery service—pizza and curry houses in particular. So opportunities now exist for van driver/owners to offer their services to these food outlets.

Are you suitable?

You obviously need to own or buy a smart-looking van. Most of the work will be at night, between 6pm and 1am, so you will need to be prepared to work unsocial hours. If you accept that then it could be a very good sideline and excellent second job.

Costs

The major cost would be the van, but also any equipment needed to keep food hot. If you get a contract from one or more food outlets, then your van will have to be clean, nicely painted and have the names of the outlets you represent on the livery. You will also need a mobile phone so that the outlets can get in touch with you immediately to give you more orders.

How much can you make?

It all depends on the contracts you negotiate with each individual outlet. If you have an exclusive contract, then that one contract will have to be high enough to make it worth your while—maybe £2 per delivered item as a carriage charge.

Marketing

The only marketing you will have to do is to sell your services to fast food and restaurant owners and managers. All that takes is a letter and a visit.

ENVELOPE STUFFING

Envelope stuffing or mail order fulfilment is an activity that is often done at home. You can work on a contract basis for a firm, or start your own service aimed at local businesses.

Are you suitable?

It can be a laborious, repetitive and monotonous job. It is okay if you don't mind that and can concentrate on stuffing for hours on end.

Costs

Nothing, just your own time.

Market research

If you intend to work for yourself, then you need to identify firms and small businesses in your area that require a regular or periodical need for envelope stuffing. Most firms these days use mailshots as a sales tool in order to drum up business. It is cheap and specific.

How much can you make?

You can usually make about £2-3 an hour for envelope stuffing, but you could negotiate a contract rate based on the number of envelopes stuffed. You might get a better rate that way. You know your own speed and you could end up stuffing 100 items for £5 an hour. Make sure, if possible, that you are paid cash in hand.

Marketing

Word of mouth helps, but so do mailshots (that is what you are selling) to local businesses and small advertisements in the local press.

FAXING

Everyone (well nearly everyone) has a telephone, but what they don't always have is a fax machine — and they sometimes need to send or receive something over a fax urgently.

Are you suitable?

You need to be happy with being housebound and, to a certain extent, machine-happy. You need to have a facsimile machine. Offering a fax service can easily be combined with an answering service, secretarial operation, home typing or word processing business, or even with another type of business. After all, if you have bought the equipment and hardly ever used it — why not make money by allowing others to make use of your machine?

Costs

The cost of a decent fax machine, a service contract (and perhaps a back-up fax machine) as well as the very expensive paper that fax machines use.

Market research

You need to live in an area where there are a lot of one-man bands — professional and creative people, and others — who can visit your home and premises to send and receive documents. You can also offer a dedicated fax mail service (if instead you have a personal computer (PC) and faxcard). Fax mail is like direct marketing but instead of posting marketing literature, it is faxed. Rather than do this manually, the faxes can be sent to a database of named people direct from a computer using a faxcard which plugs into the PC. At cheap-rate times faxes can be sent from 10p for 3 minutes. As the system is automated, once it has been sent it runs itself — dialling fax numbers and faxing literature over — so it can be run while you earn money doing other work. This will help local business people who want to reach local customers further afield at a lesser cost than sending out a paper-based mailshot.

How much can you make?

You can charge anything from 10p to 30p per transmitted page (inward or outward). If you are using the PC faxcard system, and you have a mass mailing to get out, this could add up to a tidy sum.

Marketing

You need to place advertisements, or get an editorial mention, in the local press, and put cards in local shops. A leaflet drop in your area could also be rewarding.

Pitfalls

The equipment can be very expensive, but you can offset it against tax in the first year.

FENCE ERECTING AND TREATING

Wooden fences shielding gardens from other gardens or from the road have become very popular over the years. People want more privacy, and six-foot wooden fences have come into their own. This is hardly surprising, stone and brick garden walls are very expensive to build.

But who has the patience and time to erect and treat fences? Erecting fences is a laborious job to undertake. And so many people get it wrong. They fall down, bow, or are erected haphazardly. And can many people be bothered to continue treating the wood every year or two? It wouldn't appear so.

Are you suitable?

Are you patient? Can you work in all weathers to finish the job? Most important, do you know how to erect fences?

Costs

You should expect most clients to order and buy their own fences, posts and spikes. Certainly when you start you would not be able to afford to buy and stock fences. Your expenses would be the tools for the job and woodpreservatives.

How much can you make?

You will probably find fence erecting and fence treating a seasonal job — spring, summer and autumn — but not winter. So you may find it the sort of job which you should treat as a second source of income and therefore a weekend job, unless you have an alternative winter job. But if you do well you could probably make a fair amount of money. You could charge about £25 an hour for erecting a fence and the same for treating a fence.

Market research

You need to walk and drive round your area to gauge exactly how many households have wooden fences that are in need of treating — and how many are falling down or out of line and need to be re-erected.

Marketing

Place advertisements in the local press and local telephone directories and put up notices in local shops.

Obviously word of mouth recommendations are important, but you could also leaflet the houses you have pinpointed as needing fence treatment and then call on the owners soon afterwards. But for the fence erecting side, you should approach garden centres and ask them to put up your card and notices.

FOREIGN STUDENT LODGING

There are thousands of foreign students who come over to the UK — not just London — to learn how to speak English. They usually do it for a year, before or after they go to university, or just before they embark on their chosen career. They need lodgings for that period.

Are you suitable?

You need to have a house that is comfortable and welcoming, a large enough room to let, and be in an area where students want to live.

You have to be prepared to act as guardian, friend and general homemaker for the students. You also need patience and to be flexible and understand their comings and goings. You can fit in this work with another part-time job during the hours they are out.

Costs

Time and effort. And only the day-to-day costs of providing meals, washing and ironing clothes, and cleaning their rooms. Also, they may need driving to college every day.

How much can you make?

You can earn as much as £65 a week (the maximum before you have to declare rent as income), and this works out at £260 a month, a tidy sum for not too many hours' work.

Marketing

You need to contact the accommodation offices of the colleges in your area and get your name on their lodgings list. If they are satisfied with you, then you should get a very regular supply of students to lodge.

Pitfalls

You have someone else living in your house. You may get a problem student. However, you should be able to get redress from the college if the student causes damage, and if you need to get him or her removed.

FRANCHISES

Since the British Franchise Association was launched in 1977, franchising has grown into one of the UK's most vital business sectors. You know it's a success when you see the main clearing banks and firms of accountants have set up franchise sections to assist those wanting to get into the arena, as well as those already there.

Many feel it is a good way to start your own business with a much greater chance of surviving the first three, critical years. This was confirmed by the last (1992) NatWest/British Franchise Association survey, which showed that the UK's franchising companies survived the recession better than others. Despite its success, franchising is still misunderstood by many people who often think it's just some kind of licensing deal.

What is franchising?

The franchise relationship can take many forms. Typically, it involves satellite enterprises (run by franchisees) operating under the trade name and business format of a larger organisation (the franchisor). You can buy a franchise (and become a franchisee) or form a franchise to sell to others (and become a franchisor).

And what, you may ask, is a franchisor? Good examples are Budget Rent-a-Car, McDonald's, Wimpey, Burger King, KFC (Kentucky Fried Chicken), Alfred Marks, Greenalls, Hertz, Prontoprint, Kall-Kwik, to name but a few.

Typically, it usually starts with a pilot business, which has been running successfully for a few years and doing so well that the owner of the business (franchisor) decides to expand. He figures that if it works so well why waste energy and resources opening more branches when you can sell the idea and format and let someone else do the hard work?

With this in mind, the franchisor develops the franchise operation into a duplicate of the original successful business. He may even include an operating manual to show the prospective franchisees how they can set it all up and run it, profitably. But when you've got a winning formula, it's vital to sell it to someone who will maintain and nurture it into a repeat success.

And you, the prospective buyer (or franchisee), faced with the opportunity of getting into a business that is already a success will want to know if the formula can be repeated and if it's right for you. Once you've decided on a franchise operation you need to investigate it thoroughly to ensure it is right for you. Franchises vary enormously, and some businesses don't suit everybody.

Are you suitable?

Franchises are for people who want to minimise business risk. You've bought an operation that has been tried and tested. You are probably getting ongoing help and information. You have avoided risk and gone straight into something that combines being part of a corporate business with the benefits of personal responsibility and ownership. Everything's done for you – it's as safe as any business ought to be.

The downside is that while it is your own business, you are expected to act in the best interests of the franchisor and other franchisees. One weak link will let the whole side down. It's as much in your interest to ensure everyone follows the manual, maintains the franchise's profile and image. So commitment, hard work and motivation are as important as good business sense.

Costs

On signing the contract to purchase the franchise, the buyer will usually pay an initial fee to the franchisor (which will include start-up costs). For this, the franchisor helps the franchisee set up the business – finding and fitting out suitable premises, providing stock, training, finance and perhaps help with promoting the opening.

Once the franchise is underway it's your own business but you will be expected to carry on advertising and marketing the brand name and ensuring quality matches the standards of the original pilot business. You may also pay a percentage of your monthly sales or profits to the franchisor. Or perhaps the franchisor will, instead, simply insist you buy all future product from him, and nobody else, ensuring uniformity of product, branding and customer loyalty.

The length of the contract is likely to reflect not only the type of business but also the amount of the front-end fee. The more you spend, the more you can expect reasonable security to enjoy a return on your investment of both time and money. While most contracts average five years, agreements can run from one year to 15 or more.

As well as the initial fee, the franchisor will expect to receive part of your yearly profits, based on your sales. The annual slice will probably remain constant while you struggle to maintain sales figures, perhaps faced with growing competition from other franchise operations who decide to open similar businesses to yours in the nearby vicinity.

How much can you make?

It could be said that this is very much in your hands: that the way you run the franchise will determine its success. In general, though, do franchisees make money? During the recent recession, franchise operations, like most small businesses, were quite badly affected. However, almost 60 per cent of established franchises (over five years old) are said to be satisfied with their profitability, and only 4 per cent to be making a loss.

It has to be borne in mind that while a franchise offers increased security and reduction of risk, the potential rewards are likely to be lower than running your own business. But if you are really determined to make a good profit, it is crucial that you have a sound understanding of the financial management of your operation and the required accounting procedures. A good franchisor will ensure that you receive adequate training in these areas.

Market research

When you have decided on your franchise find out how many other franchises have been sold — are there too many in one area? What kind of control is there on competition? Is there the danger of crossover between franchisees operating within one smallish area? The success of a franchise depends on its marketing by the franchisor. How much will they be spending in the coming years to maintain the brand identity?

Ask the franchisor for references. Check his company out very carefully, especially the credit ratings. Most important, do you get on well? Can you see yourself working closely with the franchisor over the coming years? Is the franchisor efficient and helpful? Just because you're buying a franchise doesn't mean you should forget the market research on your target sector or site. Look into this as carefully as if it was your own business.

In the words of the British Franchise Association 'Franchising works extremely well throughout the world, providing both Franchisor and

Franchisee discharge their responsibilities, providing that they treat each other fairly.'

Where to find more information

The British Franchise Association, Thames View, Newtown Road, Henley-on-Thames, Oxon, RG9 1HG. Tel: 0491 578050. Fax: 0491 573517 has 120 franchisor members with more than 10,000 franchised outlets in their care. Also has over 50 professional advisors (lawyers, bankers, accountants and consultants) whose experienced advice is essential to franchisees before they sign-up.

Franchise World, James House, 37 Nottingham Road, London SW17 7EA. 081-767 1371. Bi-monthly. Subscription only.

Business Franchise Magazine, Newspaper House, Tannery Lane, Penketh, Cheshire, WA5 2UD. 0925 724326. 10 issues a year, £2 each in most good newsagents.

FURNITURE ASSEMBLY

People buy ready-packed kitchen units, bedroom cupboards and other items of self-assembly furniture. Many of them don't have either the time, patience or skill needed to assemble them.

They could employ a carpenter to assemble the bigger items, but this could prove very expensive. A kitchen might cost as much as £500 (or more) to assemble and fit. A skilled person dedicated to just fitting and assembling units and furniture could provide a competitive service and undercut carpenters.

Are you suitable?

You need to be good with your hands, patient but also a fast, accurate worker. You also need to be able to work to plans—kitchen-design plans for instance. Most householders will either want to see—on site or in a photograph—work you have done, and they will prefer it if you have qualifications and are a member of a trade association.

Costs

Just the tools of the trade.

Alex wanted to be his own boss. A franchise operation.

"*I*f you're going to jump" I told him, "make sure you have a safety net."

I had taken the plunge a year or so ago and hadn't looked back. In those crucial early days my bank had been particularly supportive.

"I talked to their franchise team" I told him "and they talked me through the procedure step by step".

"Franchise team?" Alex raised his eyebrows.

"Yes" I said. "They encouraged me to prepare a business plan, so that I knew exactly where I was in terms of overheads and cash flow."

This had shown how much income I needed to generate. It was, I remember, a sobering experience.

"The good news" I told him "was that they offered to finance up to 70% of my start up costs."

"Go on" he said, with more than a hint of interest.

"Well, it wasn't just the money, it was their contacts as well."

The bank had introduced me to an accountant and a solicitor experienced in franchising. "So you see you won't be entirely on your own" I added.

"Now that you've made it" Alex asked "I suppose they treat you like any other bank?"

"Not true" I replied "The manager at my branch, came up with a complete financial package at a very acceptable price. So there are no surprises in terms of bank charges."

I paused as a rabbit ran across our path.

"But there's one thing the bank didn't give me.

He glanced sharply at me. "What's that?" he asked.

"The determination to succeed" I said.

The Royal Bank of Scotland

THERE IS A DIFFERENCE.

Call our Franchise Helpline 031-523 2178 (24 hours)

OR WRITE TO THE ROYAL BANK OF SCOTLAND plc. FREEPOST, FRANCHISE & LICENSING, PO BOX 31, EDINBURGH EH2 0DG
THE ROYAL BANK OF SCOTLAND plc. REG. OFFICE: 36 ST. ANDREW SQ, EDINBURGH EH2 2YB.REG. SCOTLAND NO.90312.

BUYING A FRANCHISE – REALISM IS THE KEY

By Ian F Doig, Franchise & Licensing Manager,
Franchise and Licensing Department in Edinburgh.

Many people dream of owning their own business but are deterred from fulfilling their ambitions because they fear the risk of failure. There is no doubt that a properly constituted business format franchise can *reduce* this risk without requiring unacceptable sacrifices in terms of independence. In short, a franchisee can benefit from the use of a proven trading name, product or service, whilst still being his own boss and has the opportunity to build up his own successful enterprise, with all of the related benefits, however realism is the *key*.

Banks will generally look to assisting in the purchase of a franchise on a ratio up to 70%/30%. In other words, if you are looking to take on a franchise from an ethical franchisor whose concept has been shown to be successful, the banks will look to lending up to 70% of the start-up costs. It is imperative therefore that the total cost of your chosen franchise is within reach. Your lending banker will be looking at your ability to service your existing commitments coupled with those of your new business so be prepared to have a full and frank discussion with your bank sooner rather than later.

Prepare well. Work out your monthly outgoings, i.e. mortgage, insurances, housekeeping, etc, to arrive at a minimum figure you require from the business to service your present commitments, and compare this figure with the anticipated profit figures for the franchise. Rework any profit figures given to allow for loan repayments, bank interest and of course your own drawing requirements. We have found that no franchisees are 'typical' and therefore it is essential that you prepare cash flow projections/profit forecasts reflecting as near as possible the 'true' costs for your unit.

So far so good – now to the franchisor/franchisee interview. This is a two-way meeting. Remember that you are also being viewed by the franchisor for suitability as an operator in the system. Have your questions ready and ensure they are answered to your satisfaction. If you take on the franchise, you will be asked to sign a Franchise Agreement. This Agreement is a legal and binding document and in every case I recommend that potential franchisees have it viewed by a solicitor with franchise experience. Similarly, I would suggest that any cash flow projections are viewed by an accountant with realism in mind. Market research supplied by the franchisor should not necessarily be accepted as provided and I would suggest that there is no substitute to you carrying out your own *local* market research which can be viewed in conjunction with that of the franchisor.

Contact as many of the existing franchisees as possible to establish if the franchisor you are dealing with is as worthy as he makes out. Check especially on back-up, support and the quality of training provided.

Finally, take your time. A good opportunity will not be lost by you fully doing your homework. Advise your bank manager as early as possible of your considerations. Listen to all advice from family, friends and the professionals, but remember, at the end of the day, it will be *your* choice whether or not to proceed. Keep the watchwords by your side: *realism*, and *affordability*. Be self-critical and ask these questions of yourself – can I afford the franchise, and am I being realistic in my ambitions?

The Royal Bank has produced a booklet to assist when considering buying a franchise entitled 'Franchisees'. Copies are available free from The Royal Bank of Scotland, Franchise and Licensing Department, 42 St Andrew Square, Edinburgh EH2 2YE (telephone 031-523 2178).

WHO ARE ESSO PETROLEUM?

Recognised as market leader in Petroleum Retailing in the UK, Esso supplies approximately one fifth of the market through its chain of 2,350 Service Stations.

Two thirds of our UK volume is sold through the 1000 of these Service Stations which are owned by Esso and run by licensed operators.

It is these high volume sites where the new Snack and Shop convenience stores are really setting a fast pace as customers, not just motorists, realise that they provide a very convenient facility for shopping around the clock.

The new style convenience stores sell groceries (one of the highest growing sectors), newspapers, magazines, confectionery, flowers and a fast developing range of snacks and drinks. Microwave ovens enable customers to heat-up pies and pastries, drink dispensers offer tea and coffee. Almost 100 outlets now have their own in-store bakery offering fresh baked breads and pastries and self service quick fried snacks such as chips, pizzas and chicken nuggets.

WHAT SORT OF PEOPLE IS ESSO LOOKING FOR?

Esso is seeking dynamic men and women to run their Service Stations who are: committed to hands-on retailing, understand the value of merchandising, are interested in people, good administrators and are safety conscious.

THE INVESTMENT

As well as the right aptitude a potential Esso licensee also needs sufficient working capital. The Esso organisation retains ownership of the sites and fittings, but the licensee has to finance all stock, including fuel supplies. The working capital required for this can total between £25,000 to £50,000.

However, there is a less expensive alternative. In London and along the M4 corridor there are Service Stations run by Dart Oil (a wholly-owned Esso subsidiary). Fuel at these locations is the responsibility of Dart Oil and the operators (known as commission agents) only have to purchase the shop stock which is normally valued at between £10,000 to £15,000.

There is one major plus point to investing in an Esso Service Station which differentiates our package from many other business opportunities. Because the capital invested is used to fund stock, should the Licensee decide to cancel his agreement with Esso, the full fuel stock and any appropriate shop stock may be purchased by the incoming Licensee. In this manner, a high proportion of the capital investment may be recouped.

Ironically the recession has helped Esso recruit some excellent new retailers. Early retirement and redundancy has led many people with managerial expertise, with Blue Chip companies/Banks and Armed Services into Forecourt Retailing with Esso.

Successful applicants undergo a 14 day residential training course which covers the many aspects of Service Station retailing.

A significant proportion of Esso licensees earn in excess of £25,000 per annum after all expenses are paid, based on the profit margin of the motor fuel sales and a share in the shop profits and other ancillaries such as the very profitable car washes. A Dart Oil commission agent can expect a forecast income of anything from £15,000 per annum to in excess of £20,000.

And everyone has the backing of a company which has a proven track record. Esso, who have been trading in the UK for over 100 years, sell more fuel than any other company and aim to move their Snack & Shop convenience store chain to the same No.1 position across the whole retail sector, not just forecourts, by 1995.

WHERE DOES ESSO NEED PEOPLE?

Opportunities are available throughout the UK so for further details of the Esso Deal, why not write to: **Recruitment Co-Ordinator, PO Box 268, Edgware, Middlesex HA8 6HE**

THIS USED TO BE A PILE OF RUBBISH

NOW IT'S WORTH £12,000

Every day a huge number of spent ink, ribbon and toner cartridges similar to those above, are thrown away by businesses throughout the country simply to be replaced by new ones.

We can offer an alternative Remanufacturing and Recycling.

The spent cartridges in the picture, having been recycled, are now worth £12,000 and the end user will save a further £12,000 against the cost of replacing them with new ones - a good deal for all, including the environment!

We have perfected a system which can recycle almost all office and computer printing consumables. If its a ribbon, a cartridge or even an ink pad we can recycle it and save the end user 30%-70% of the replacement cost.

In addition, we guarantee that the recycled product will equal or even exceed the manufacturer's quality and all our products are covered by full product liability insurance.

Ribbon Revival are now making their 'know how' and expertise available to entrepreneurs worldwide through a new franchise arrangement. Launched in 1993, a substantial number of franchises have already been established in the U.K. and in the Channel Islands, Hong Kong, and South Africa.

Ribbon Revival Ltd., Caslon Court, Pitronnerie Road, St. Peter Port, Guernsey, Channel Islands, GY1 2RW, Great Britain. Tel: 0481 729552 Fax: 0481 729554

The company:

White Knight was formed in 1989. Now a group of companies providing a range of services to small business clients. The original service was based on the preparation of VAT returns.

The service:

Principally our clients are retail traders. Newsagents, Grocers, Village and Corner Shops. H M Customs and Excise provide fifteen alternative methods of calculating VAT for a retailer! We are able to calculate from all the possible options and advise on the most appropriate. Savings of hundreds of pounds per quarter are common.

We provide:

Full initial and ongoing training, at our headquarters until you are ready to work from your chosen base (home or office). Operations and Marketing are fully covered. There is no limit to the time spent training. We operate at your pace and from your current knowledge. 24 hour technical helpline and full support manuals also come with the package. All future upgrades, enhancements and amendments are included.

You provide:

IBM compatible computer and printer (cost approx £1,000 if not already owned). The ability and enthusiasm to offer a professional service to a defined market place. Numeracy and literacy are required, but accounting and VAT knowledge is not!

*A profitable, professional future awaits you
as a White Knight Franchisee. Owning and
operating a VAT Accounting Bureau.*

Phone (0823) 251223

The cost:

Initial charges for an exclusive countywide area, are
£8,000 plus VAT. Royalties of 10% of turnover are also
payable.

You can be:

A Sole Trader, Partnership, or Limited Company.

The next step:

Telephone or write for an information pack and sample
VAT return.

White Knight Franchising (UK) Limited
Hi Point, Thomas Street, Taunton, Somerset TA2 6HB.
Telephone (0823) 251223 Facsimile (0823) 330970

Drink To A Successful Future...
with a Coffilta Coffee Franchise

THE COMPANY
Established in the 1970's as a coffee machine manufacturer, we now offer a wide range of beverage products, machines and ancillaries in the form of a complete distribution package supplying hotels, restaurants, cafés, offices, etc. via a national network of Coffilta Coffee Distributors. Our distribution package includes an exclusive area for sales development, full training and sales support.

THE PRODUCT RANGE — Coffilta Coffee Services supply a distinctive range of top quality fresh roast and ground coffee produced, packed and supplied from our own processing house in the attractive Coffilta packaging. We offer a free, on-loan equipment service for pour over coffee's plus ancillary products such as non-dairy creamers, sugar sachets, cafetières, cups, spoons, stirrers, hotel room packs and chocolate mints. Add our latest range of In-Cup machines and In-Cup products and you can see why our distributors have so many opportunities to establish a customer base.

THE SERVICE –– By investing time recruiting and training people we are able to quickly establish a new distributor into an exclusive area, equipped with the knowledge, products and sales approach that will enable them to open new accounts and maintain them by providing that personal, local service that is essential in building a strong customer relationship and looking after their repeat order requirements.

Our executive distribution package will cost you £6,500. You will receive an initial 2 days comprehensive training programme, on-site training, telesales, canvassing support, administrative support, coffee machines and samples plus a business starter kit.

If you would like to know more about this exciting business opportunity contact me, Peter Carlile, Coffilta Coffee Service, Halesfield 14, Telford, Shropshire, TF7 4QR. Telephone: 0952 680404 for free information pack.

COFFILTA COFFEE

Coffilta is a company that sells both coffee and coffee machines through its distributorship of franchisees. Established for over 20 years as a coffee machine manufacturer, it has now built a reputation for supplying top quality coffees and ancillary products.

Established in the early 1970's as a manufacturer of catering coffee filter machines, Coffilta quickly established a reputation for quality. The company set out its plans to develop sales through a network of distributors and moved the business away from pure manfacture towards a complete coffee service, able to look after the requirement of cafes, restaurants, hotels and offices; indeed any type of outlet where good coffee was to be appreciated.

More to Offer Today's operation is flourishing and boasts 42 distributors throughout the UK. The product range has developed to include coffees, catering teas, cafeterias, sugars, creamers, espresso coffees, bulk brew packs and full support products, point-of-sale material and sales literature. Peter Carlile, since taking over in January 1991, has set about improving the company's profile, product range and distributor package. The operation is leaner than before, with operating costs and overheads kept to the minimum, allowing Peter to invest in distributor recruitment and development, and introduce new systems such as the Coffilta In-cup machine and branded product range.

Distributor Support Each Coffilta distributor receives a two day intitial training course with accommodation and meals provided, on-going sales and administrative support, a business starter pack, use of a tele-sales and mailshot facility and promotional sales literature. All distributors have a credit account from day one, products and machines are delivered without charge to the distributor usually within three days of order. Local and national meetings are arranged and encouraged between distributors with up-date letters, information and the Coffilta Newsletter issued at regular intervals. The company endeavours to generate sales leads by telephone canvassing, mail shot letters, some national advertising and support, and will on behalf of the distributors, make approaches to hotel chains and breweries, etc. For further information contact: Peter Carlile on 0952 680404.

FROM STITCHES TO RICHES

The rapidly increasing interest in needlecraft as a hobby has given rise to a new concept in retailing – rising far above the old-fashioned corner-shop image.

'The Stitch Shop', a self-styled 'needleworkers paradise' in its beautiful Port Solent marina location, is the front runner in a new breed in needlecraft shops.

The needlecraft industry has changed beyond recognition, expanding nearly 40% over the past few years, mainly due to the phenomenal interest in cross stitch and needlework kits, which had their origin in the United States.

Back in 1988, one couple saw the potential in the market, and now run 'The Stitch Shop', the largest pure needlework shop in the South of England, attracting regular customers from as far afield as Scotland. With sales increasing at the rate of 31% a year, they decided that the way forward was to franchise the concept.

Lesley Harris and Mike Davis spent nearly two years researching and preparing for franchising 'The Stitch Shop' under the guidance of the Centre for Franchise marketing, and have put together an impressive package for a minimum capital requirement of £20,000 from the franchisee.

They look for an individual or a couple with a highly commercial approach to running their own business. They will then find premises, fit out and stock the shop, carry out all the buying and provide comprehensive training based on their combined 30 years of experience in the trade.

The rewards are not only financial, but have the added bonus of being involved in the fascinating world of crafts.

For further information, contact The Stitch Shop, Tel: 0705 321102

Greencare:
The laser cartridge recyclers

Greencare Ltd, the unique new franchise launched in October 1993, offers the chance to become involved in Europe's fastest growing business sector and is set to become the largest laser cartridge recycler in UK.

The UK laser cartridge market is currently worth £210 million, although at the moment less than 10% of these are recycled. Projections to 1995 value the market at about £400 million with recycling forecast to rise to between 20-25 per cent. This represents a huge business opportunity for those wishing to make money and to be associated with a dynamic enterprise.

Based on the simple idea of completely remanufacturing costly laser printer cartridges and reselling at a fraction of the original price, Greencare provide large organisations with an efficient method of dealing with technical waste (ie: laser cartridges, typewriter ribbons, fax cassettes and toner from copier cartridges); help them save money and assist with conservation of global resources.

It allows companies to conform to recent 'Duty of Care' legislation under the 1990 Environmental Protection Act which outlines responsibilities for the disposal of technical waste in a proper, controlled and suitably recorded manner.

Quality of products and service are key to Greencare's success. Greencare offer a free delivery and collection service. Products are logged into a central computer system by bar code reader at the customer's site.

Operating under strict quality control systems, cartridges are remanufactured to a standard often exceeding the original product specification and undergo individual testing.

The Greencare network will be made up of more than 80 franchise territories, each operating in its own exclusive licenced local area with a minimum of 1,000 potential customers each; with a turnover of more than £1/2 million; and employing more than 10 people.

Following a stringent selection process, all Greencare franchisees undergo an intensive training programme.

The initial franchise fee is just £8,000 with equipment and working capital set at a maximum of £18,000. The contract includes a Greencare liveried van, computer, fax and telephone links to head office, and central sales and marketing support.

Linked to the head office computer network, a Greencare franchisee can enjoy the pleasure of running his or her own business without the administrative or financial burden of billings, credit control or bad debts.

Greencare offers the best for both worlds, personal service that only a committed local company can give it's customers - and a range of recycled products that satisfy the emerging awareness of most companies to their environmental duties.

Greencare Limited, The Old Saw Mill, Sharpness, Gloucestershire GL13 9UN
Tel: 0453 511366   Fax: 0453 511714

Autosheen are the U.K.'s largest mobile valeting franchise. Founded in 1984 the company has successfully exploited the growing demand for skilled valeting in both private and corporate markets. Numbered among its clients now are such household names as BMW (GB) Ltd, Porsche Cars (GB), Budget-Rent-a-Car, Digital and English Nature.

The combination of thorough training and extensive marketing support have helped to ensure Autosheens success in a very competitive marketplace. As with any successful franchise, it has achieved this by a combination of good quality franchisees, and continual assistance from Head Office.

This assistance takes several forms; the provision of good quality point of sale material, a comprehensive insurance package that covers all eventualities, tie-ups with several leading chemical suppliers and contacts with some of the country's major manufacturers and importers. All this allows the franchisee to get on and develop his business knowing he has a powerful support package behind him, plus the benefit of a well known brand name.

"Providing a high quality service in this business is fundamental", says Graham Bullock, Autosheen's Marketing Director, "and by service we don't just mean the ability to valet vehicles. It is also appreciating the importance of correct marketing, such as customer prospect and follow up systems, full insurance cover, and correct use of chemicals. Failure to understand these points is the main reason why people who start this business on their own fail so quickly. It is because we do provide these services that our rate of success is so high".

How much can you make?

You could earn £50-100 a day (and maybe more, if you market it as a premium service), as you could finish a wardrobe, bedroom unit or kitchen in a couple of days.

Qualifications

You need basic carpentry skills, and formal qualifications will certainly help.

Market research

Very little—you just have to feel that there is a market for this service in your area. However, an area with period houses, many of which may need new kitchens or bedroom cupboards, is best for this type of service.

Marketing

Leaflet houses in the area and advertise your services in the local press and telephone directories—*Yellow Pages* and Thomson's local directory.

You could also approach major furniture chains that supply fitted furniture, and try to get on their approved supplier lists, and work direct for them as an approved fitter of bedroom furniture and kitchens. They would then probably take a commission, but at least you would be guaranteed extra business in addition to the work you generate yourself.

FURNITURE REMOVALS

Are you suitable?

If you like driving, don't mind lugging furniture and chattels (you might need a helper), and you have a half-decent van that is clean and tidy, then you could be in business.

Costs

Just the van and travel expenses. You should take out insurance to protect yourself in case of an accident, damage to goods and theft.

Market research

You need to target or live in an area where there are a lot of people living in rented flats. In particular, one where there are a lot of students or young couples who don't need a national removals firm with sizeable lorries to move their small collection of worldly goods. Perhaps they are prepared to hire your service to take their goods to another part of the area or back home rather than go through all the rigmarole of hiring a van themselves and packing their goods.

How much can you make?

You must be able to compete with the van hire firms. Check their daily rates for hiring a van and match or undercut, or add a premium according to what you think the market can take.

Marketing

Get signs placed in local university student union halls, in shop windows, and advertise your service in the local press.

Pitfalls

If you rely too heavily on students and young couples for your business, then one week you could have a rush of activity, and then nothing for several weeks. You have to be prepared for this swings-and-round-abouts type of working.

GARDENING

Gardening is another of those occupations that depends and relies on people not having the time to do it themselves. Luckily, there are millions of people who neither have the time nor the skills to design or tend to their gardens, but still love having a garden to enjoy.

Are you suitable?

You have to decide whether you intend to offer a gardening upkeep service or contract gardening, which will include an element of design and skill. You are more likely to make a decent living out of contract gardening, but then you need knowledge of garden design and planting.

Whatever the case, you need to enjoy the outdoors and be prepared to do all the routine jobs such as mowing, pruning, planting, and sowing that a garden requires.

Costs

Although most people with large gardens have their own tools and equipment, you may need more. You should have your own equipment including lawn mowers and a whole selection of gardening tools. You also need a mini-van or large car to cart them around in.

How much can you earn?

You can earn anything up to £10 an hour for offering a full contract gardening service.

Marketing and market research

Only professional people and couples aged 30 plus with large gardens and no time for gardening would be interested in your service.

Most work initially would come from friends and friends of friends. You could try on-the-spot checks of the area you intend to work in to see which gardens are in desperate need of tending, and then dropping leaflets through their letterboxes with details of your service.

Future

If you find that you are in demand more and more for your gardening services, then you could expand and take staff on, and offer your services to the business sector on contract.

Pitfalls

During a recession, gardening is one of the first services that people dispense with. It is not an essential service. Also, gardening tends to be a seasonal occupation — winters can be quiet.

Gardening — market gardening and nurseries

You can do worse than make money out of your garden. But you do need to have a large garden to make a living out of growing vegetables, fruit, and plants. The garden must also have good access to the road if you want to sell some of the produce from your house.

Are you suitable?

You need to be a very enthusiastic and experienced gardener, and you need to be prepared to work in all weather conditions, otherwise your business could flounder.

Costs

You need a suitable van, all the necessary gardening tools and equipment (which are not cheap) and raw materials — seeds, saplings, plants, and so on. You also need a good-sized greenhouse for plants, vegetables, and fruit that need protecting against the cold weather, and to start plants off. A secondhand greenhouse could cost you more than £1,000. And you have to remember that it costs a lot of money to heat a greenhouse.

How much can you make?

If your produce is good, and you find markets for it, then you could make a very good living. But for most it will be a case of a few pounds on the side.

Qualifications

You could brush up on your skills before you start your business by getting a National Vocational Qualification or a Diploma in

Horticultural Studies. Or you could go on a part-time course at a horticultural college.

Market research

You have to be in an area that doesn't have a nursery or market gardening operation.

Marketing

Where to sell your produce? You can offer local greengrocers and flower shops some of your vegetables, fruit, and plants and flowers at discount rates. You could also become an emergency supplier.

If you decide to sell your produce from your house, then you need to advertise your services in the local press and leaflet the local area. Beware though, you may need planning permission from your local authority to operate a sales operation from your home.

Alternatively, you could sell your produce on a market stall or on a good site at the side of a road.

Where to find more information

Horticultural Trades Association
Horticultural House
19 High Street
Theale
Reading
Berkshire RG7 5AH
0734 303132

Gardening — grass cutting

There are many busy people, professionals in particular, who just do not have time to cut their grass. They don't need a full gardening service, but they do have a large lawn that needs cutting once a week or fortnight.

Costs

You just need a vehicle of some sort that can transport a diesel or electric lawnmower, and ancillary tools like trimmers.

Market research

Find out if there are enough people in your area or in a neighbouring area who fit your potential client description, and express an interest in your service. As long as there are not too many people with their own gardeners, or who do all their gardening themselves, then you could be in business.

How much can you make?

This will depend largely on the number of clients. You could treat this job as a weekend only job, and fill your Saturdays and Sundays with a diary of people so that you can go from job to job.

Marketing

The best way to market your service is word of mouth, but as you get more into the job, you could also put advertisements in local newspapers, put cards in local newsagents' windows, and put leaflets through people's doors.

Pitfalls

Little work during the winter — you would have to do something else or rely on your weekday job (if you have one).

GREETING CARDS

Designing and producing greeting cards has become a boom business over the last ten years. Shops have sprung up in every high street, and the choice of cards has increased substantially. You can now buy cards for every occasion and humorous cards make up the majority of those sold.

Are you suitable?

You need to have good design and illustration skills, a spark of imagination, and if necessary, a sense of humour. If you have another skill — such as flower pressing, lacemaking or embroidery — you could make very special cards for sale through local gift or craft shops.

Costs

Just time and materials to produce the cards. If you produce them yourself, then you will have to invest in design, print, and distribution.

How much can you earn?

If you design and produce your own cards you may struggle, but if you sell your ideas for royalties on sales to a dedicated greetings card manufacturer, then you could earn a substantial amount of money if your cards prove to be popular.

Qualifications

It helps if you have a background in art. Either do an evening class or get training from an art college. However, your success will depend more on your originality, quality of work, and your ability to sell your cards than on a technical qualification.

Market research

Roam around card shops and newsagents, and take note of the designs and types of cards that sell. Buy an assortment and study them closely to get an appreciation of what makes them attract buyers. Then see if you can come up with original ideas. Test them out on your friends. You may prefer to design 'classy' cards rather than humorous ones.

Marketing

If you go it alone, then it will be up to you to organise the printing of the cards, and up to you to sell them. You can sell them through local shops, by mail order, to charities (as specially designed issues), through the newsagents and office trade press, and through off-the-page coupon advertisements in the national press.

Or you could focus your marketing on the main greeting card producing companies by approaching them direct. You may get turned down several times before getting any sort of interest.

GUTTER CLEARING

If you have a head for heights then why not consider gutter clearing as a service? It is an essential job that has be done throughout the year, but few householders get round to doing it for themselves.

Costs

What you need is a van, a long ladder, and cleaning rods, which could all be bought for less than £1000.

Market research

Find out how many local people need their gutters done by someone else at least once or twice a year. If the response is good, then you could go into business. Also, find out whether you need extra insurance cover should you get injured. It is a hazardous business. It may also be wise for you to have an assistant to help with the ladders and make sure the ladder is secure.

How much can you make?

You will have to test the market, the price range should be from about £20 to £50 per job. It is best combined with other services such as gardening or window cleaning to make it viable.

Marketing

Once you have established a small network of clients — friends, relatives and recommendations — you should move one step further and widen your business. You can do this by putting advertisements in *Yellow Pages* and in the local press, and by getting cards and leaflets printed and dropped through local residents' doors.

Pitfalls

You probably wouldn't be able to make much of a living during the winter, or the windy and wet months.

HAMPERS

Designing a hamper is an art in itself. You have to know what makes a balanced hamper, and each hamper has to suit the occasion.

Hampers are popular all year round, but particularly during the 'Season' (Henley, Goodwood, Royal Ascot, The Derby, Glyndebourne, Wimbledon), the summer months, and at Christmas.

Are you suitable?

To design mouth-watering food hampers you have to have good gastronomic taste. Do you know what should go into a Christmas hamper? The answer is: brandy butter, plum pudding, tinned ham, bottles of sherry, port, and claret (and any other complementary delicacies).

Fresh food hampers demand even more creative input, and to compete your hampers must not only look good but be competitively priced.

Costs

Sufficient stock at the right time of year to fulfil orders. This can run into hundreds of pounds if the items to go into the hampers is of a very high quality.

As a result it's best to produce a catalogue and make up hampers to order so you do not have expensive stock lying around. Costs can be cut by making arrangements with wholesalers.

How much can you earn?

This depends very much on whether you are offering a local fresh food hamper service, or selling non-perishable hampers. It also depends on the competition in the market.

Market research

If you are selling locally, you have to ensure that there is a need for such a service. Are there speciality shops, delicatessens and butchers who would be prepared to buy and sell, or put one on display with your card attached?

Equally, if you intend to set up a national service, you need to know who else is in the market. You have to scan the business and marketing trade press, the grocery trade press, national newspapers and consumer magazines.

Marketing

This very much depends on whether you are selling locally or nationally. If you are selling to a local market, you need to approach local traders to convince them of the idea of your fresh food hampers for particular events. You could also take a stall and sell your hampers at local fairs and agricultural shows.

You could also advertise your services in the local and regional press, county magazines (if you live in the country), and in local shops.

If however, you intend to produce and sell non-perishable food and drink hampers, then you need to place advertisements in the national press, the upmarket and consumer press such as the Lady, Tatler and Country Life.

Businesses are keen to give staff hampers as 'Christmas bonuses', so this market can be tapped through advertisements in the business and marketing trade press.

Pitfalls

Not being able to sell fresh food hampers in sufficient quantities, and therefore being left with a lot of wasted food. Equally, being left with too many unsold and costly non-perishable hampers. This business is very risky for this reason alone.

HEDGETRIMMING

Although not everyone has a hedge—many people prefer to have wrought iron or wooden fences—enough people in large houses and suburban areas do have them, so hedgetrimming could be a worthwhile service to provide to the local community.

Are you suitable?

You need to like the great, healthy outdoors and have a steady hand to form a neat hedge. If you think you have enough creativity to progress to more ornamental hedges, all well and good as it could increase your worth.

Costs

All you need is a vehicle to take away hedgecuttings (or you could burn them on site—but that's not very environmentally friendly) and a hedgetrimmer and saws.

How much can you make?

You could make about £15 to £20 an hour in the right area. Start small, and work over weekends to build up business gradually.

Market research

Go round your area and see if there are sufficient hedges to be cut. You could be competing with DIY gardeners and hired gardeners.

Marketing

The best way of picking up business for this kind of work is literally to walk round the area you have decided on to find work. See which houses have hedges and bushes that are in need of cutting. Knock on doors and offer your services. If they take you on and you do a good job, you should be able to get repeat business and more work through recommendations.

Future

If you do well, then you could expand your area or diversify into an allied trade.

HOUSE-MINDING

People who go away on holiday, on short-term leave, or to a new home, often have no one to look after their property. They need a person or company they can trust to check on their home while it is empty. They could go to an expensive fully-fledged security firm to oversee the property or ask a neighbour (who may or may not be reliable) to look in from time to time. Or... they could employ a house-minder.

Are you suitable?

You need to be reliable, conscientious, and probably a nosey-parker. Your job is to check that no burglary occurs, but if it does, then to know what to do in the event and deal with the situation. You might also be hired to look after a pet, water the plants (see also the section on Plant Care and Hire), turn lights on and off, take in the post, check the answerphone for messages, and deal with any other crises — burst pipes, roof leaks, and so on.

Cost

Nothing, apart from transport if sites are remote.

How much can you make?

If you offer a premium service, then you could earn as much as £50 a day (or even more) per person if you are also offering a comprehensive package.

Market research

At first you would want to start as a sole trader, so you would need to operate in an area where there are a lot of wealthy people who need your type of houseminding service.

Billbusters!

Revealing a new opportunity in helping companies to avoid overcharging by public utilities billing

Has your company ever been overcharged through errors in billing from the privatised utilities like telephone, gas, electricity and water – and even by your bank?

Barry Thornton of Bank & Utility Cost Analysts (BUCA) believes that it's very likely, if his experiences in helping clients to detect their overcharging are anything to go by.

He points to reports in the media which suggest that British businesses in aggregate have been paying up to £100 million a year more than necessary, thanks to inaccurate billing.

Stephen Alambritis of the Federation of Small Businesses complains that this factor must be a contribution to many thousands of small businesses going to the wall in recent years.

"Overcharging is a hidden resource loss which needs to be urgently monitored and rectified," says Thornton, who is now inviting applications for professionals to join his company to be trained as cost analyst Affiliates. "Our system, pioneered in the USA, analyses clients' utilities and bank accounts, often going back several years to detect errors. With one client in the hospitality industry, we have recently located errors to the value of £15,000."

Once the overcharging has been detected by a BUCA Affiliate, explains Thornton, applications, usually successful, are made to recover the overpaid amounts – from which the Affiliate draws 50% and an agreement to continue monitoring the bills over a period of 48 months. Once several clients are secured, says Thornton, the Affiliate's business becomes "extremely profitable."

An additional investment project and service planned by BUCA is running its own gas utility company to provide cheaper fuel.

Thornton suspects that the gradual introduction of water meters is going to compound the overcharging risk, pointing to one client whose water bills since meter installation have risen astronomically – from a previous £1,000 to £10,000 a year.

"What people tend to ignore," says Thornton, "is that there are many steps involved in the preparation of a bill, all of them subject to human or computer error, from an inaccurate reading to someone keying in the wrong information. There are so many risk stages, so many opportunities for utilities and banks to end up charging more money than they deserve. Our task is to monitor accounts and redress the balance. Companies have enough pressures on them nowadays without the added burden of overcharging."

What surprises him is that whereas in the USA, BUCA Affiliates came from various career backgrounds including automotive sales, in the UK, there is almost exclusive response from the professional classes – Chartered Accountants, lawyers and management consultants.

"The calibre of Affiliates is much higher over here," he observes. "It's a very attractive and satisfying business to those types of people – work where you act as a consultant and have to use your brain analysing trend graphs and sensitivity indices. It's one of the very few genuinely white collar opportunities on the market."

Although the recruitment for Affiliates only began in June, he reports, 10-15 will already be operational around the country by the late Autumn. "Interest has certainly been aroused, so we expect to be taking on many more Affiliates in the last quarter and then well into 1994.

"And there's plenty of business out there for our Affiliates. Every firm uses a bank or utility company and is therefore a potential customer – and both analyst and client can share in recovered savings going back as far as the client makes his records available for inspection, and into the future, often taking a total of 96 months or more in which to detect errors. Even small businesses can yield big returns – like one public house where overcharging of £17,000 was detected. It's a fact – Bank and Utility Cost Analysis is the white collar business of the 1990s."

Marketing

Word of mouth and recommendations would be essential to your success, and the only other type of promotion you would need to undertake would be advertising in the local press.

Future

You could set up a network of house-minders and just run the business. You would then become the manager and organiser of staff and need to advertise more extensively in publications like *The Lady, Country Life* and *Tatler,* and in the national press.

HOUSE-SITTING

House-sitting is related to house-minding, only you actually live-in while the occupants are away. They could be away for as long as a year.

This is less of an occupation but more a way of living in a nice home at no rent. Many people allow friends to house-sit. But if they don't need to rent it out and need a trustworthy person, they may have to find one.

You could start a business as a broker or agent of house-sitters. But you will need to register as an employment agency, and have the responsibility of thoroughly checking out your staff.

Are you suitable?

You need to have good administrative skills and present yourself well to start a house-sitting agency.

Cost

The cost of a phone and phonecalls. And time, lots of time.

How much can you make?

You will get your money by charging the occupant a small fee for arranging, vetting, and introducing suitable candidates. And you would charge a house-sitter a higher fee (in lieu of rent). So you could make about £500 straight commission per deal.

Your responsibilities would end there. Your job has been to match-make.

Market research

Difficult, or almost impossible to do.

Marketing

Advertising in the national or regional press in the accommodation sections. This would be to attract owners as well as potential house-sitters.

Pitfalls

A lot of wasted money on advertising with very little return. A lack of participants. Long periods without earning a commission.

INDEXING

Indexing in publishing tends to be a freelance trade. To be a good indexer you have to understand the main themes of the book and to organise the index by key words: people, events, subject matter and so on.

Are you suitable?

You need patience and attention to detail. You also need to be a vigilant reader and have the ability to work to a publisher's or author's brief. It is an arduous but much required job.

How much can you make?

A qualified and experienced indexer can make about £10 an hour. You need regular work to make it pay. So you will no doubt have another job in publishing.

Pitfalls

You won't get much work unless you keep in, and network with, publishers and authors.

Where to get more information

The Society of Indexers operates a registered index for experienced indexers.

The Society of Indexers
38 Rochester Road
London NW1 9JJ
071-916 7809

LAUNDRY

A local home laundry service on the doorstep would be the answer to many a busy couple's problems. Professional couples, and couples who both work but have children, hate facing up to household chores, and to some, washing and ironing are the most laborious and time-consuming chores of all.

Are you suitable?

If you have worked for a laundrette or dry cleaners you will know what you're doing. If not, then you have to be prepared to work hard and fast for your clients. You need to be able to iron well. Men in particular want crisp, well-pressed shirts.

Costs

You need a roomy kitchen or utility room, and a very large washing machine and a powerful tumble dryer. You also need two irons (one a steam iron) and an ironing board. All that should come to no more than about £700. Insurance, in case you ruin clothes, is also recommended. Then there is the cost of detergents, hot water and electricity.

How much can you make?

If you get about five to ten regular clients you could charge them each about £10 for a large load, washed and ironed. So multiply that by 20 and you are talking about £200 a week (or more). The time consuming element is the ironing. You can charge more if you do a really professional job and present your pressed clothes nicely, and offer a collection and delivery service.

Market research

Start by asking your friends if they need a home laundry service and see if they would be prepared to recommend you to their friends and neighbours.

Marketing

You could be very cheeky and stand outside laundries and dry cleaners in the area and hand people leaflets with details of your home laundry service as they enter or leave these shops. Instead, you should put notices in local shops and newsagents, and advertise your services in the local press.

Future

If you do well, you could expand into a business unit, move from being self-employed to a small business, take on staff and develop your business still further. You could then offer your services further afield. But you would need to advertise in glossy consumer magazines and buy delivery vans.

LEAFLET, BROCHURE AND PAPER DISTRIBUTION

In the last 20 years there has been significant growth in the amount of paper and newspapers that is shoved through letterboxes.

More and more business people have not only switched to direct mail as a way of getting their message direct to consumers, but have also realised the potential of leaflet drops to inform customers of new services. Leaflets are particularly important for local businesses. Equally there has been substantial growth in the number of hand-delivered 'Freesheet' newspapers.

Are you suitable?

Can you walk for mile upon mile delivering leaflets, brochures and freesheets? Can you work during the day, or at night, or at weekends? Can you cope with bad weather? Those are the requirements of this job.

How much can you make?

Normal rates for leaflet distributors can be anything from £2.50 an hour to around £6.00 an hour. Or £18 a thousand to £40 a thousand. Most people should be able to deliver 100 to 200 leaflets an hour. You get employment through leaflet distribution companies.

The best way you can make money is to become a team leader and own a car or van to carry colleagues in. That way you can cover a wider area.

You need to register with a number of leaflet distribution companies to ensure regular work for you and your team.

Or better still, set up on your own and approach local minicab firms, restaurants, home improvement companies, and shops and offer your services at a competitive rate.

Paper boys who deliver daily papers can get 40p per household a week, or around £15 a week.

Pitfalls

The money tends to be poor. If you are going to deliver your own leaflets or business cards, why not make cash doing it by delivering for firms too? This might help solve the problem of waiting for more work when times are slack.

MARKET TRADING

Market traders who are sole-traders do not always have the easiest time. It is a tough life. You have to rise very early and work till quite late in the afternoon. To be successful you have to rely on your own judgement and initiative.

There are many different types of market stall: council operated or privately operated, outdoor and indoor without permanent units, indoor with permanent units, weekdays and Saturdays and Sundays — and specialists in antiques, crafts, and so on.

Are you suitable?

Taking these problems into account, you also have to be aware that you will not obtain a regular stall or pitch in an established market without first attending as a casual. This can be hard. A casual trader has to be prepared to stand in queues early in the morning hoping that a stall is available. The longer you attend the more chance you have of being allocated a regular stall when one comes available. Only families that have been there for years can pass their stall down to their kin. Can you hack it, through thick and thin?

Costs

A sturdy van is essential if you need to pull a mobile market stall. Although the majority of markets do supply stalls, some do not, so you will probably have to purchase a market stall through the trade press. Hiring a stall or site normally costs about £15 a day (but this figure does vary according to area and part of the country).

How much can you make?

If you have hit upon a lucrative line of goods — perhaps clothes, fruit and veg, household goods or even antiques — then a market stall can be very rewarding financially. You have to specialise.

Regulations

Large stores may stay open for six hours on a Sunday and small ones can stay open all day. There are no more restrictions on markets.

Food traders, particularly those selling perishable goods, have to adhere to the food hygiene legislation, which includes statutory temperature controls for selling and transporting foods.

You have to abide by the strict consumer legislation, Acts such as the Sale of Goods Act and the Trade Descriptions Act. (Car boot sales at the moment are not covered by such Acts.)

Where to find more information

You can become a member of the National Market Traders' Association. The NMTA represents its members on political issues, provides legal advice and insurance.

The National Market Traders' Association
Hampton House
Hawshaw Lane
Hoyland
Barnsley S74 0HA
0226 749021

MODELLING

Modelling is often a part-time occupation until models have established themselves. You don't get well paid unless you get picked as the 'face', and then, like waif-like young supermodel Kate Moss, you can earn millions.

But for others modelling is just another way to make extra money. Many will have other roles — they could be housewives, actors or whatever who get called on to do modelling jobs from time to time. You have to be totally committed to modelling to make a full-time success of it.

Are you suitable?

You need be prepared to work hard and long unsocial hours. You also need to have an interesting feature that art directors and model agencies require: a striking or beautiful face; a lived-in face, full of character; beautiful hands or legs. But some agencies specialise in 'ordinary' people for crowd shots. If you have time on your hands it may be worth registering to see what comes up. You could even put your children or pets on a model agency's books.

Costs

To get onto a model agency's books you need to get professionally taken shots taken of your face (or other features) and send one off to your list of top agencies.

How much can you make?

If you reach the top, or are able to get regular work, you can earn in excess of £300 or more a day. The market for models is huge. You could break into the catwalk scene, or do work for magazines, posters, and TV commercials.

Some of the best paid work is for modelling abroad where you can earn twice the fees you would get in the UK. However, most models do not earn anything like this amount.

Remember you do need to belong to a model agency, and as such you forfeit at least 5 per cent of your commissions to the agency.

Pitfalls

No work.

Where to find more information

The Association of Model Agents represents the interests of model agencies. It is a good first stop for aspiring models.

The Association of Model Agents
The Clock House
St. Catherines Mews
London SW3
071-584 6466

MULTI-LEVEL MARKETING

Multi-level marketing, also known as MLM or network marketing, is a means of selling goods and services that is becoming increasingly popular in the UK.

MLM originally appeared as 'pyramid selling' in the early 1970s and was discredited through a rash of abuses by unscrupulous operators.

Fortunately, the industry is now controlled by tight legislation and is legal and ethical.

How does it work?

First, participants or 'distributors' have to join a trading scheme and then pay for goods or services from the company (or other participant) who runs it. What sets MLM apart from traditional sales methods is the fact that participants can also make money from recruiting others into the scheme.

They can also earn commissions or fees on sales made by other participants 'down the line', or boost their commissions or fees when elevated to a higher level within the scheme (usually as a result of achieving a set sales target), or from fees and payments for training other participants.

Properly managed, an MLM scheme can create a self-supporting selling organisation with a distinctive style and brand image, and tends to attract strongly motivated, self-employed people who are good at selling – either themselves, or goods and services.

Your first encounter with MLM will probably come via an advertisement in a local shop window or newspaper, a friend or through your letter box. It's up to you to decide if MLM should be used to raise extra cash when you need it, or turn into a full-time occupation. Either way, your earnings may be taxable.

Are you suitable?

It helps if you have had some experience in sales, marketing or promotion. Are you confident that you can really sell the product or service and that there are lots of people who want to pay the asking price? If there are too many distributors in one area trying to sell the same thing, you may find yourself in a discount war.

What kind of boss are you? Do you think you can find people to help build your MLM scheme? Can you motivate all the participants you recruit (who will then report to you) so that they will get out there and sell? Because if no one is selling anything, you won't make any money. Moreover, are you well-organised and efficient? You need to be reasonably numerate and able to handle paperwork. Presentation is important, too, if you are dealing directly with the public, so ensure that your appearance is smart and clean.

Cost

It is illegal for any scheme to ask for money, goods or services before a contract is signed. However, once enrolled as a distributor you will be asked to pay an initial fee. The maximum amount which may be legally accepted is £75.

In most MLM schemes, participants buy the product from the company at a set ('wholesale') price and sell it at a profit. If you get in from the start (unlikely) you could make money from recruiting new people and earning commission on their sales, which increases as the levels build and multiply – sale upon sale upon sale.

Remember you'll almost certainly be working long hours, from home. You could be selling products, recruiting people and training the (ideally) growing number of people who will work under you. They'll want information, stock, help with their recruitment, training and a bit of encouragement from time to time.

You'll need a car, an answerphone (or someone to take calls while you're out 'on the road'), energy, resilience, bags of confidence, a thick skin (for the many rejections all sales people experience) and a good sense of humour.

Some believe that later entrants may not do so well as they may find it difficult to recruit extra people. And the number of sales of most products or services is often rapidly overtaken by the larger number of participants or distributors trying to sell in the same area.

Others claim that MLM is an inverted pyramid where everybody starts at the bottom and has the opportunity to build a large organisation — some many times larger than his or her sponsor's (the person who recruited them and who they answer to) organisation.

How much can you make?

Some believe that MLM probably offers the opportunity for wealth to more people than any other form of business. Thousands of people have reached millionaire status by taking advantage of the concept. But only after a great deal of dedication, motivation, and hard work.

Like you, they were attracted by the possibility of a high income from part-time work, the chance to start and build a new business without any previous experience, low overheads and minimal financial risk (that's provided you've done your homework very carefully).

Market research

You need to know if there's an existing and growing demand for the scheme's product or service. Properly run schemes will normally invest in market research and should be able to back up any statements they make on potential growth.

Check on the size of the MLM you have been invited to join. How long has it been running? Are you near the top or the bottom? Ask to meet several people who can tell you honestly how well they have done. And how many other participants are operating in your chosen area.

And are you fully aware of the requirements of the Consumer Protection Act, the Sale of Goods Act and guarantees offered by the manufacturer? And if you are self-employed have you considered National Insurance, Tax, VAT etc?

Where to find more information

An advice sheet, 'Multi Level and Network Marketing', and free booklet, 'Multi Level Selling Schemes: a Guide to the Pyramid Selling Schemes Legislation', are available from the Department of Trade and Industry, Consumer Affairs, Division 3b, 10-18 Victoria Street, London SW1H 0N; 071-215 3342.

NAPPY DELIVERY SERVICE

If you have a baby of your own, you know how expensive disposable nappies can be and how many you (or rather your baby) can get through in the course of a day, week and month — loads!

So why not help yourself while helping others? Make a business out of buying nappies in bulk and selling them on by delivering them to mothers' homes.

Are you suitable?

This would probably suit women more than men, because by and large you would be selling to mothers who would be more comfortable dealing with a woman rather than a man. You need enough dry storage space to store nappies — a converted spare room would be the ideal solution at first. You should also have the ability to sell — even if it is to local mothers at the nursery.

The Immobiliser

A-160 Security monitor

Brace Door protector

The ELERT series

The VA 190 and remote

The PAAL Series

Unprecedented Growth - Unprecedented Potential

Quorum International has achieved unprecedented network marketing growth in North America and is presently establishing a strong base in the United Kingdom, ready to propel itself into Europe.

WANT TO KNOW MORE ?

Just phone : 0908 - 368868
We will co-ordinate
an introduction

Quorum™
Securing Life

The Quorum International Business Opportunity

The impact of rising crime statistics is clear – personal and property protection is becoming a must for people in all walks of life, to ensure security and peace of mind.

Quorum International is a powerful new force in the marketing of electronic security devices, offering a range of advanced but low cost products that matches people's needs today.

The range includes personal security alarms, designed to attach to people and/or their possessions, with a pull-cord activated distress siren in the event of attack.

Portable property alarms for articles such as luggage, sports equipment and personal computers are proving increasingly popular. Armed and disarmed with a personal code number, these advanced products are activated through sensitive movement detectors.

The Quorum range also includes easy-to-install alarm systems for cars and homes, based upon technology that detects sub-sonic shock waves created by forced entry through external doors and windows. These alarms are available with remote control operation, and remote sounders to satisfy the most diverse consumer needs.

The company is an integral part of the Applied Electronics Group, a major manufacturer of electronic products that also supplies key components to well known producers including Texas Instruments, Commodore, Philips and Fisher Price.

Originally established in 1976, the Applied Electronics manufacturing organisation employs over 4,000 people in Hong Kong and the Republic of China, where over 60,000 electronic components and finished products are produced every day.

The Holding Company went public in 1986, since when it has enjoyed notable success on the Hong Kong stock exchange.

Having developed its current range of security products, Applied chose to adopt a network marketing policy to allow distribution directly to the end user – hence the formation of Quorum International.

The initial operations were focused in North America, where a network of over 250,000 distributors was created within two years. Based upon this success Quorum established a UK operation in 1992 which has already developed over 20,000 distributors – a number that is rapidly increasing.

The launch of a Dutch operation in November 1993 will further increase Quorum's international coverage, and will create significant opportunities for distributors to broaden their own personal networks, boosting their earning potential and expanding market coverage.

Quorum International will develop additional European markets over the next eighteen months to expand its network. This policy will ensure significant business opportunities for its existing distributor base.

Multi-level network marketing is not a new concept. However the unique relationship between Quorum and Applied Electronics, that is the relationship between distribution network and manufacturer, sets a new standard in the industry.

In short it means that Distributors in the Quorum network can look forward to a very long term business opportunity, both through ever-widening geographical coverage and a fast changing product portfolio.

Markét development is both rapid and totally effective – because the financial strength of the Applied group provides a strong foundation for growth.

The long term stability of Quorum International is assured – not just through financial support but through the continuous development of advanced new products, and the emphasis on retailing.

Today's range is oriented around society's need for effective security products. Tomorrow's Quorum range will reflect tomorrow's needs – from advanced home electronic devices to voice activated entertainment systems, and more!

Herbalife Positioned for Success

Marketing gurus will tell you that there are 3 great keys for successful retailing - position, position, and position. One UK Company today is positioned for continuing and future success.

Herbalife celebrates its 10th anniversary in the United Kingdom in the next few months. Most of its competitors are either out of business or fledgling start-up operations. Herbalife seems to have achieved that magical balance between experience and longevity on the one hand, and freshness and vitality on the other.

Herbalife was founded on the California dream of young Mark Hughes back in 1980. At the start of the 80's his introduction to the marketplace of a revolutionary concept in weight control products caught the imagination of the accepting California public. The Company that he formed has remained innovate ever since, providing a product mix from the best that is available in both nature and modern technology.

Today Herbalife trades in 17 countries around the globe with continuing expansion plans targeted to take the Company into another dozen new countries this year. The Company's international growth has not come by corporate design alone. it appears that Herbalife's unique marketing plan has become the catalyst for the Company's continuing success. Unlike its competitors in the direct selling field, Herbalife seems to have developed a marketing plan that allows direct compensation to be paid to its distributors on their own international business. The difficulties caused by exchange controls, legal challenges and the complexities of international business are all absorbed by the company for the benefit of the distributor.

Whether Herbalife positioned itself in the health and nutrition industry by total design, or whether it was just pure luck it was certainly the right choice. Herbalife's now world-acclaimed nutrition products are positioned in one of the fastest growing industry sectors. In addition, the high consumability of the Company's products generates a consistent demand from loyal customers. The Company's distributors can choose to create new customers, service existing customers or both.

The stated aim of President and CEO, Mark Hughes, to the shareholders of his publicly listed Company has attracted ever increasing shareholder interest, and consequently, share price. Whether Mark achieves his aim of "taking good health and nutrition, country by country, and language by language right around the world", time will only tell. As far as positioning is concerned, Herbalife certainly appears to be the right Company with the right product in the right place, and at the right time.

All readers of
"Making Money"

Please take the time to read the display advertisement on the right hand page. I'm sure you'll find it of considerable interest to say the least!

In fact, you're probably reading this AFTER you've read the ad already. Why is that? Why did the headline catch your eye quite the way it did? Why was the diagonal flash the second thing you noticed? Why did you look at my signature before reading this?

The answers are really very simple – your eyes scanned these pages in an almost identical way to EVERYONE who reads them. Know how a prospect will read a page and you can construct it to present YOUR sales message in THE most powerful way.

Detailed guidelines on how to prepare marketing material that really works for you is given in "I've Just Got To Have One!", the first title that you will receive under **Breakout!**, our new publishing initiative.

Breakout! is a truly international business that offers independent agents the opportunity to sell high quality, really usable, books to an eager public. Information is the ultimate commodity, and GOOD information will always find eager buyers.

If you are looking for a high profit, low outlay, easy to run business that offers very real growth potential then I strongly urge you to send off the reply slip opposite. We'll send you full details by return. The address is Freepost so you don't even have to find the cost of a stamp!

Best regards,

CHRIS PAY

THE MARKETING NETWORK

Chancery House, 1 Effingham Street ♦ Ramsgate, Kent CT11 9AT
Tel: 0843-852723 ♦ Fax: 0843-852721
A Nexos business

"How to cut your mortgage payments in half (or even more!)"

The FACTS You Must Know

Written by an insider who's been helping clients for years to dramatically reduce their mortgage bills. A MUST read!

Which is easiest - to earn more money, or to pay less out?

This Kogan Page/Daily Express book is jam-packed full of exciting new businesses that you can start NOW to make more money, full time or part time. But have you ever thought, I mean REALLY thought, about WHY you want to earn more money?

A great chunk of most people's monthly income goes on paying off a mortgage. It's the largest debt most of us ever take on, and certainly leaves many running simply to keep up with the outgoings. But what if there were ways to dramatically reduce that burden and make the whole thing much more manageable?

Fortunately there are ways - lots of them - but only a few are known or seriously considered by those taking out a mortgage. Some consultants know these "tricks of the trade" and help their clients to structure their mortgages in the most effective way. One such has written a blockbuster of a new book on how to go about reducing YOUR monthly outgoings - "How To Cut Your Mortgage Payments In Half (Or Even More!)."

Even after starting with a mortgage it is still possible to arrange things to your benefit. All you need is "the knowledge" of what to do. This book will give you that - and more!

What about both?

"How To Cut Your Mortgage Payments In Half (Or Even More!)" is available EXCLUSIVELY from agents for **Breakout!** , the publishing initiative from The Marketing Network. Other titles available within **Breakout!** cover a wide range of subjects, each of them vital to achieving success today.

Content, layout, illustration and presentation are always of the highest possible quality, making these books that people like to buy AND sell! You can be involved NOW and in at the start of what look set to be record sales. For FREE details please fill in the slip and send off to our FREEPOST address. We'll return your action pack the same day.

YES, I want to stay ahead and obtain full details NOW!

Tell me about Breakout! and the opportunity as soon as possible.

Name ....

Address ....

....

Postcode ....

Tel. No: ....

Please cut out, or copy, and send to:-

**The Marketing Network
(11013KP)
FREEPOST 600
Ramsgate
Kent
CT11 8BR**

Network Marketing is proven to be the most powerful method of distributing products by enabling huge numbers of people to be profitably involved in the business. Ultimately, whatever marketing method is being used, people must want to buy the products which therefore must provide 'Good value for money'.

This is never more important than with Network Marketing because distributors are heavily reliant on the benefits of the product to secure sales and to interest people to join as new distributors. The vast majority of distributors are not 'natural' sales people and employ their personal enthusiasm, excitement and belief in the product in order to succeed.

Finding a product that people need is often considered the key. 'I've just got to have one' is what every Distributor wants to hear. Timing also is most important. Today every one needs to stretch the pound in their pocket just as far as it will go which isn't too far once the essentials have been paid for. A product that substantially reduces high expenditures on those essentials is a necessity. By also addressing everyone's desire to help the environment the timing is doubly powerful.

Saving money and helping the environment very rarely go hand in hand but a newly introduced electronic fuel saving device, developed by the British company E7 Limited, helps home owners and businesses reduce the size of their heating bills substantially by using less fuel without any loss of comfort or hot water in the process.

E7 Limited guarantees to repay the full cost if fuel bills are not reduced by 20% in the first year. Typical installations yield impressive savings well in excess of this figure. Results from a large number of installations prove performance and are well documented. Sussex University confirms that installation can reduce fuel bills by around 30% while at the same time making a serious reduction in the amount of carbon dioxide being released into the world's fragile atmosphere.

All installations are relatively simple involving no plumbing or mess requiring only electrical connections. Installation is carried out by a subsidiary of THORN EMI which also endorses the product.

Other benefits of installation include extended boiler life by reducing wear and tear significantly thus helping to save on expensive boiler maintenance. The unit can be detached and fitted to another boiler if the owner moves house, something that can't be done with cavity wall insulation or double glazing.

This newly established network provides distributors with unparalleled potential to earn substantial incomes. With a market of 30 million installed boilers plus increasing fuel costs and taxes it is easy to see why this business opportunity is so powerful. The compensation plan is extremely rewarding and all company trainings and support is freely given. Call E7 Limited now 0424 733566.

ENVIROTECH INTERNATIONAL - Your Pathway to Success.

During the past three years Envirotech International has become one of the fastest growing Network Marketing companies in the world. Early in 1991, when Envirotech opened for business, the company had only one product, one distributor and one country to work in. Today, less than three years later, Envirotech International has: marketing operations in thirty two countries around the world; 40,000 distributors in the U.S.A. alone; Network Marketing operations in five countries - UK, USA, Canada, Mexico and Norway, with Denmark, Sweden, and Ireland coming on stream in the Spring of 1994; and a range of five highly successful products, In fact, Envirotech International's network marketing operation has grown at a rate exceeding six thousand percent per annum during the past three years and, as a Network Marketing company, this growth has been achieved by solely personal recommendation- something must be really outstanding about this company!

Why are Envirotech employees and distributors proud of their Company, their Products and their Opportunity? Why has Envirotech grown by personal recommendation? Why have Envirotech grown by over six thousand per cent per year during the past three years? It is simply because Envirotech International have;

- **the best products and the best opportunity** in the Network Marketing Industry,

- **products which provide the best demonstration** in the History of Direct Sales; you just let the sales person out of the bottle!

- **an enviable reputation as a World Leader** in the development of waterless technology and water saving products. Envirotech's renowned development programme is providing products today which promise a better tomorrow,

- **products which are relevant today:** the current use and depletion of the earths most precious resource - water - is leading to the next environmental crises (National Geographic Special Report),

- **genuinely unique products:** technologically and in use they outperform any other product of a similar kind,

- **products which save time and money,** and

- **a genuinely unlimited market:** everyone can use Envirotech's products which are both consumable and repeatable.

Envirotech's income opportunity is available to anyone regardless of age, sex,creed, race, or financial circumstances. From the successful entrepreneur to the student, housewife or someone who has retired or is seeking a new full time, or part time career, Envirotech has an opportunity to meet all aspirations.

The Company's opportunity is backed by international, national, regional and local training and support from the Company, experienced distributors and leaders in th eindustry.
You are invited to step onto Envirotech's Pathway to Success: experience a product demonstration and learn a little more about the Envirotech business. If what you see and hear makes good sense you may like to join the growing Envirotech family- if it's not quite for you- that's 'alright you may wish to try the Envirotech and become a satisfied customer.

35 years ago, Nutri-Metics International was founded on the concept of achieving good health and natural beauty, through nature itself.

Today, Nutri-Metics, derived from the words **Nutri**tional Cos**metics**, continues to answer the growing world-wide demand for naturally wholesome health and beauty products. With an extensive range of high performance skin care, personal care, colour and health care products. All inspired by the best ingredients nature has to offer. And sold through a network of 200,000 Consultants world-wide. This highly personalised form of distribution has resulted in outstanding customer loyalty, with 80% of sales coming from repeat business.

Nutri-Metics International is a privately-owned Australian company and a world leader in direct selling, with operations in 16 countries across Asia, Australasia, North America and Europe.

Not only do we have all the ingredients for a beautiful skin, we also have all the ingredients for a great business!

If you're looking to simply supplement your existing income, or to secure your future by creating a national and international organisation, the Nutri-Metics International Business Plan offers a highly rewarding financial and lifestyle career, for all walks of life.

Whether you're a homemaker or a professional, the Nutri-Metics International Business Plan gives you the choice of investing a few hours each week or making your Nutri-Metics business your total career. This allows you flexible working hours and the freedom to operate from

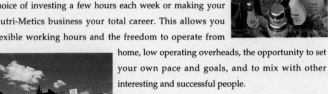

home, low operating overheads, the opportunity to set your own pace and goals, and to mix with other interesting and successful people.

Most importantly, you'll have more time to yourself and your family.

If you would like more information on Nutri-Metics, please call 0908-262020 or write to: The Sales Manager, Nutri-Metics International (U.K.) Ltd, 3 Garamonde Drive, Wymbush, Milton Keynes MK8 8DF.

The *BACCHANALIA* Bandwagon!!!
With a feast of easy-to-sell goodies!!!

BRUSHLINE
- *Already proven Network Marketing and Direct Selling market*
- *The finest up-market Cosmetic, Artist, Dressing Table and Equestrian brushes, as well as a super range of general brushes for the home*
- The highest quality available in Direct Selling
- At prices 10%-20% below competitors
- And a range at least *ten times* as big!

GREEN GODDESS COSMETICS
- *Fantastic Quality for price:* for example, our quality of lipsticks at £4.25, other companies sell at £7-£11!
- *No animal products:* not even the hairs of the brushes! Ideal for Vegans
- *Cruelty free* as certified by the British Anti-vivisection Society

WINE'S FUN WINES
- Select your wines the *WINE'S FUN* way, buying what you like, when you like, from the shop in your living room!
- *Over 150 wines from all over the world*
- *Carefully chosen by a specialist wine importer*
- *From £3.30 to – anything you like*
- For those of you who like variety, *you need have only* one *of each label!*

BACCHANALIA FINE SPICES
- ★ *Pure and unadulterated spices*
- ★ *Carefully chosen, by experts from around the world, for their fresh aroma*
- ★ *Over 55 popular herbs and spices to tempt the gourmet*
- ★ *Unquestionably the most attractive bottles on the market, based on the classic, clean lines of a Greek column, make this an exceptionally welcome gift*

DEVON SPRINGS WATER
The best Passive Income ever seen in the UK! All you do is find the customer – then receive 20% commission for the rest of your life (whilst still registered), *for doing nothing!*
- ⊗ *Free delivery direct to home*
- ⊗ *Top quality at only 45p per litre*
- ⊗ *Revolutionary packaging means* fresh water for three months after opening!
- ⊗ *Environmentally friendly.* No bulky bottles to dispose of
- ⊗ *Recycleable packaging*
- ⊗ *Ideal for boats, caravans*
- ⊗ *Commercial offices.* Slash spring water costs!

☆ **Network Marketeers and Party Planners needed all over the UK** ☆

DEVON SPRINGS WATER also needs non-MLM Distributors for *genuinely exclusive* areas!! Phone now on 0291 628787. *BACCHANALIA* Holdings PLC.

Mail Boxes Etc.(MBE), the worlds largest network of Postal, Business and Communication Centres, has over 2,000 of their unique franchised retail outlets in 11 countries.

This high street revolution offers 'One-Stop-Shop' convenience and flexibilty to local residents and businesses. As a Postal Alternative an MBE Centre Provides all the Royal Mail Products and Services excepting registered Mail. There are no queues, no bars and an MBE customer can expect to receive friendly and efficient service. With facilities to send and recieve Faxes, Photocopying, Personalised Mailbox Services, Stationery, Business services such as Printing, Word processing, Laminating and Binding, Mail Boxes Etc. caters for all those essential needs.

In association with The Royal Mail, Parcel Force, UPS, TNT, DHL, Federal Express and other recognised carriers, MBE are confident that they can get any package, anywhere at any time and probably do it cheaper. They also provide custom packing and packaging supplies.

All franchisees have the option to add on any products and services which enhance their image as a Postal, Business and Communication provider, depending upon their own abilities and the market in which they operate. Examples of which include instant signs, accountancy services, Rubber Stamps and Engraving, Secretarial Services, Company Formation & Registration, Gift Wrapping and Greeting Cards, Phone-messaging, Etc. Etc. Etc.

Ron G. Holland author of the international bestseller Talk and Grow Rich was asked to do a motivational talk at the beginning of 1993 to the Bizeq key networkers that had flown in from all over the world. When he saw the incredible product known as The Listener (a burglar alarm that protects a complete home for around £200) he knew he would be able to offer an unrivalled business opportunity to the thousands of people worldwide that had read his books. Ron has always maintained that you can create wealth without capital and to join Bizeq and get a showcase full of products costs you less than £400. That will get you started in a business that has the potential to lead you to financial freedom.

Ron has spent the last six months travelling extensively all over the world as sales and Marketing Director for Bizeq Ltd. He has done Spain, France, Sweden, Norway, Belgium the USA and Ireland and over thirty thousand miles in his fully loaded seven series BMW in the UK.

Bizeq goes from strength to strength and now operates out of twenty-two countries. The product range includes home alarms, car alarms and personal alarms, as well as an alarm that will protect garden sheds, sliding doors and computer and office equipment.

Bizeq are the Sponsors of Crimestoppers on Meridian Television and will be doing all they can to help communities to reduce crime. To this end they will be appealing to industry to create more jobs, encourage communities to set up more youth clubs and will be working with parents to develop stronger family roots with their children. They will also be developing a Junior Crimestoppers Club.

Ron has just launched a brand new book entitled Turbo Success which is all about goal accomplishment and success. It is tremendously powerful material and contains the mind power tricks that has led to fabulous success of many of his readers as well as the power that enabled him to walk across a bed of red hot coals on the Ray Martin Midday show while he was promoting his book in Australia. What was truly amazing about that feat was that he actually got Ray Martin himself to walk on the coals by putting a program into his mind that took three minutes flat. That stunt not only jammed the switch boards for three hours but also sold a lot of books. This is one book you must read! It is available from Bizeq.

NEW IN THE UK
Turn your computer to gold!

With a package of 12 different horoscopes, the only one of its kind in the world!

Now let your computer earn extra money for you!

Pegastar is a comprehensive business concept, consider the following features which will help ensure your success:

- worldwide exclusive software package
- 12 analyses assiduously collated from ancient cultures
- hotline for all questions
- readymade mailings, posters and visiting cards
- huge market potential

- over 10 years experience
- high profit potential
- small initial investment - minimum risk
- start as a second job - maintain security of first job
- be your own boss

Seminar Presentations

We would like to invite you, without commitment on your part, to attend one of our forthcoming information seminars. We will explain all aspects of this business opportunity, applications, market, etc., and how over 1,500 users in (continental) Europe are already using the concept.

If you complete and return the coupon below you will receive an information pack and an invitation to a presentation near you.

✂ -

INFORMATION REQUEST FORM

☐ Please send me an information pack

Title (Mr, Ms, etc.)	First name	Last Name

Address

	Postcode	Tel:

Please complete and return to:
Pegastar SA, 108 New Bond Street, London W1Y 9AA, or, direct to our head office,
Pegastar SA, Le Château, CH-2028 Vaumarcus, Switzerland (tel: 01041 38 553434, fax: 01041 38 553262).

Turn your computer into gold...

...with our computer personality analysis package, the only one of its kind in the world!

With over 1,000 partners in 8 countries, PEGASTAR is now the market leader worldwide in the field of computer personality analysis.

PEGASTAR puts the focus on people as individuals: We're not a faceless corporate giant, but a community of real human beings with a desire to share our know-how to make life easier for others. We help you to develop a secure existence to guarantee your own future!

No. 1 – We're the world market leader!

The PEGASTAR business plan is a straightforward and economical method for combining entrepreneurial drive and a desire for independence; the low initial investment means your risk is minimal whilst the profit potential is enormous!

PEGASTAR is a very special type of business – it's not only a simple and proven way to develop a successful, independent business, it's also one of the best ways to make high profits with a small investment. We don't supply **just** software, we provide you with a complete business concept! With over 10 years' experience, you'll be backed by a strong partner to help you launch your new business.

The only software package of its kind in the world!

The PEGASTAR business plan provides you with a complete software package, the only one of its kind in the world, with programs for scientific analysis (PSYCHOGRAM), parascientific analysis (COSMOGRAM) and partnership analysis (PARTNERGRAM). These programs are already available in several languages.

Sophisticated business plan

PEGASTAR is a cooperative marketing system. Close cooperation between the partners – licensor and licensee – creates a powerful, highly-competitive combination whose effectiveness guarantees its success.

We offer you: a product, a brand, an image and an identity, market experience, advantageous purchasing terms, a highly developed administrative concept, individual training on request, high-calibre advertising materials at low cost, nationwide advertising, initial and advanced training courses.

From you, we expect a willingness to work hard, an initial capital investment and the ability to apply your own initiative to the market.

Our support services include a hotline, upgrades, in-house magazine, market test reports and further training seminars.

As a PEGASTAR partner, you will be able develop your full professional and personal potential; with the PEGASTAR TEAM to help you off to a flying start!

Unlimited applications

Just think of the opportunities for using the PEGASTAR concept: high-calibre advertising materials to make selling easier, leaflets for mailings, newspaper and magazine inserts, small ads, advertising features (we even have our own advertising pool), brochure racks, fairs and exhibitions, department stores, shopping malls, cooperation with other businesses, hiring out the complete computer system, mail shots, cooperation with seminar organizers and many, many more.

Minimum costs – Maximum profits

PEGASTAR provides you with an exceptionally profitable product. Don't believe us? Just take this example: let's say you sell flirt and erotic horoscopes at a special price of $7.50/£4.50 each: your material costs for 8 pages of paper – just a few cents/pence!

Low investment – Low risk

Starting your own business normally requires a high time and financial investment and often special training. Whilst franchise concepts normally start at around $10,000/£6,500 (on average over $25,000/£15,000), with PEGASTAR you can start building your own independent business with only a small amount of start-up capital. Just ask for our program licensing agreement to discover the prices for yourself.

Extra tax benefits

Home computers are often used for only a few minutes a day; but now your computer can open up undreamt-of possibilities. Registering yourself as a business may allow you to claim your computer against tax, and the same may apply to part of your home (office), your car, entertainment expenses etc.

Make your computer work for you!

Be your own boss!

As a PEGASTAR partner, you can develop your full professional and personal potential! Our partners usually start on a part-time basis, retaining the security of their full-time job. What you get out of being a PEGASTAR partner is up to you, but remember, you are not alone, the PEGASTAR TEAM is right behind you!

In September this year, PrimeTime Health & Beauty launched a unique, new range of high quality, value-for-money personal care products in Britain.

Although new to this country, the management team behind the company is vastly experienced having spent over 20 years in direct multi-level marketing world-wide, including the markets of South Africa, Japan, the USA and across continental Europe.

Recruitment of the network of independent consultants necessary to service its proposed nationwide organisation is already well under way, with PrimeTime willing to offer the opportunity of becoming trained distributors to as many people as possible.

The belief is that it really will be of benefit to those who either use the products to improve their own well-being or to contribute to the happiness and welfare of others by recommending them to their family and friends.

Introduced under the *"Essentials"* brand name, the range consists of Health, Beauty and Skin Care products, each formulated by a combination of herbalists, pharmacists, nutritionists and beauty therapists using only the purest of ingredients, such as natural plant, fruit and mineral extracts.

The complete *"Essentials"* range is available exclusively through the distributor network and cannot be bought in High Street shops or any other conventional retail outlet.

Of particular interest, to many consultants and customers alike, is the company's concern for the environment. None of its products is tested on animals or includes animal derivatives in its formulations and every care is taken to use materials which are either recycled or recyclable in the selection of product packaging.

One of PrimeTime's first priorities has been to initiate an extensive research programme to formulate a selection of new products intended to extend the range by catering specifically for special-interest consumers such as women, men, small children and more mature adults.

For those considering life as a consultant, much of the appeal is the change it offers to be your own boss, with the personal freedom and flexibility to choose when you work and how much you earn.

The options are to build a business for yourself on a part-time basis with the additional income paying for the extra luxuries you've always wanted.

Or, if you choose, to turn the opportunity into a full-time and highly lucrative alternative career, working towards establishing your own financial security and independence.

Previous commercial experience or indeed educational qualifications are not as important as the willingness to take advantage of comprehensive training and support programmes which are provided free of charge.

To get the best from your PrimeTime opportunity, be prepared to take positive action, become involved, meet interesting people, attend exciting events, travel both locally and abroad, meet new challenges and have a lot of fun.

Qualifying to become a consultant gives you the opportunity to develop your latent abilities, enjoy a better lifestyle, achieve your dreams and fulfil your ambitions by being both recognised and financially rewarded for your efforts.

Not bad for a day's work.

Technical Development (UK) Ltd are the manufacturers of Ecoflow, a fuel saving device using magnetic induction. There are three models of the product: Ecoflow 1 for all types of combustion engine up to 7 litres capacity. Ecoflow 2 for combustion engines greater than 7 litres capacity and to eliminate scaling of plumbing in hard water areas. Ecoflow 3 for all types of gas or oil fired boilers.

All Ecoflows decrease the amount of fuel consumed and reduce the harmful emissions produced from burning fossil fuels. Technical Development (UK) Ltd have numerous endorsements from various sources (inc plc's) held on record, plus Ecoflow 1 has been subjected to an independent test by a Government Laboratory which proved its effectiveness beyond doubt.

Technical Development (UK) only markets Ecoflow through the Company's independent distributors. Their profit plan is acknowledged as one of the fairest in the MLM industry as it does not incorporate any time scales, ongoing qualifications and all positions are permanent once achieved.

The market for Ecoflow is enormous, ranging from cars and boats through to domestic boilers and industrial heaters. This is Network Marketing in its truest form with all products being distributed direct from the factory to the sales force with no middle men at all.

The Company was established in 1991, many of its distributors have already built very successful sales teams but with such a vast market-place sales growth is set to continue for many years.

Costs

You first have to register your business as a company in order to qualify for a card to buy in bulk from wholesalers. But the real costs are the
bulk buying itself. You need to buy sufficient quantities of nappies to
qualify for bulk discounts. This could run to hundreds of pounds initially.

You also need a big enough car or van to transport the nappies,
and you need a large load to bring down the transport cost when you
undertake a delivery round. But just as essential, you need to be well-
organised and keep a diary, so that you know which mothers require a
renewal of stock each week.

Try and make sure that you receive cash for any transaction where
possible. Otherwise you could get too many bad debts and that could
cripple your business in its infancy.

How much can you make?

If you build up a good circle of users locally, then widen the circle to
include surrounding districts, you should make a good enough living

HOW TO PROSPER FROM SLUMP TO BOOM
INTO THE FOREVER LIVING NATURAL UPWAVE

Mr Dustin Greene, The Company Managing Director, talks to Richard Williams

It has been a very busy few months for Mr Dustin Greene, Managing Director for the UK end of Forever Living Products, the US natural consumer products business best known for its unique aloe vera products.

In quick succession, the company has announced plans to expand into countries around the world. They have accomplished massive international expansion since 1983, and are No 1 in their field in 26 countries, with the UK expected to become the 27th, says Mr Greene.

Mr Greene has been with Forever Living since starting out as a distributor 13 years ago. He has a disarmingly informal style and irreverant sense of humour and obviously enjoys his pioneering position as the growth accelerates towards the billion dollar annual retail sales goal.

This company is responsible for creating millionaires amongst its distributor force and Mr Greene expects to see similar earnings for some people in the UK and Europe.

This is no get rich quick scheme, Greene is quick to point out. The company takes the risk element away from our network of independent distributors by operating product centres and offices through a team of Area Sales Managers appointed by the company.

In line with Mr Greene's mission he is currently negotiating for a prestigious stately home style training centre on the M40 corridor, and a London product centre.

---

out of it — and cover the costs of your own child's nappies at least! Your gain is the difference between the cost you buy the nappies at wholesale, less transport costs, and the amount you sell them for.

Market research

This could prove difficult to gauge at first. You could find out how many ante-natal and post-natal groups operate in the area and how many births are registered on average at the local hospital. You would also need to identify how many nurseries and playschools are located in your area.

Marketing

You would have to send letters with details of your services to local GPs and midwives and to the administrators of ante-natal and birth departments of the local hospital. Where possible you would need to ask these people if you could put up notices in their surgeries, offices and departments. You also need to do the same with creches, nurseries and playgroups, and again inform them of your services.

Obviously, you could advertise your services in the local press. Word of mouth is the most potent way of gaining new business.

Pitfalls

If you do not shift enough stock then you might be left with hundreds of pounds of unsold stock. But looking on the bright side, as long as you have a baby of your own you will at least be able to use the nappies up in due course — and you did buy them at a discount. Your baby won't want for dry nappies. But provided you build up a regular list of customers, you buy to demand.

Future

If your nappy delivery business is successful, you could provide a full baby service which could include deliveries of talcum powder, powdered milk, and so on. (See section on Bulk Buying and Selling).

NUDE MODELLING

Believe it or not you can get paid for sitting around. It's called nude modelling for serious artists and sculptors.

Are you suitable?

If you are bashful, you can forget it. However, you needn't have the 'perfect body'. In fact if you have interesting features — facial or body — then you will probably be even more acceptable. Also, most artists prefer fatter models.

You need to be prepared to strip off completely and sit in a room for anything from two to five hours at a time in front of five or more artists. You also need patience and an ability to sit reasonably still for a long period of time.

How much can you make?

In London, you can get a flat fee of £7.50 an hour. You get paid by the London Institute, the umbrella organisation in charge of all art colleges in London, although you have to contact each individual college for work. You can expect to get about 20 per cent less at art colleges outside London.

Pitfalls

Sitting for hours on end, sometimes in the freezing cold, and being bored.

PAINTING AND DECORATING

Are you suitable?

If you don't mind the fumes and you have a head for heights, then painting and decorating could be for you.

How much can you make?

The sky's the limit. If you work hard and get your business up and running efficiently, then you can make a reasonable living or earn a good bit of extra cash on the side. There is always a great demand for good painters and decorators, particularly ones who have vision and a spark of creativity.

Costs

All you need is a van, a ladder, materials (brushes, paint, wallpaper, etc), and trade insurance.

Health & safety

A booklet entitled 'Health & Safety in Painting' is published by the National Federation of Painting and Decorating Contractors and written with the regulations of the Health & Safety at Work Act in mind. You can also get guideline publications on handling paint safely and scaling buildings from the BSI (British Standards Institution). Tel: 071-629 9000

Qualifications

These are not essential but you will need a degree of skill. If you don't do a good enough job, householders may not pay up.

Pitfalls

Working on the outside of buildings in mid-winter, or inside in scorching hot weather.

Where to find more information

The National Federation of Painting and Decorating Contractors (NFPDC) is the leading organisation representing painters and decorators in the UK. It represents large and small contractors. The NFPDC is itself a member of the larger Building Employers Confederation (BEC).

NFPDC
82 New Cavendish Street
London W1M 8AD
071-580 5588

PARTY PLANNING AND SELLING

Party planning has many other names, the most respectable being direct selling, but it is also known as network marketing and multi-level marketing (in the past it was called pyramid selling).

What is party planning? Ever heard of a Tupperware party? This is where a self-employed agent representing a certain company organises parties where clients can come and inspect the goods on offer and buy.

Direct selling works this way. You join at a certain level. Part of your commission for selling goods goes up the line to the person who recruited you and in turn to those who recruited them. When you recruit for people below you, then you receive a percentage of their commission and it then goes up the line. People at the top of ladder make the most money, and in theory at least can become very rich indeed.

You get those below you to host a party, pick up the orders and then you get your commission. Your role is not only to sell as many goods as possible, but to recruit more and more people below you to sell so you can earn a percentage of their sales.

Are you suitable?

You need to be confident, thick skinned and probably driven by money (or the need for money), because what you are usually selling — household goods, jewellery, clothing, water filters and cosmetics — is rarely exciting and might not turn you on (except for Anne Summers which now sells its sex-aids and lingerie through parties).

Costs

You have to make sure you do not buy stock from your supplier company. The most you should buy is a start-up demonstration kit. Direct selling organisations who insist that you buy their stock should be avoided like the plague. You don't want to be left with hundreds of pounds worth of goods you cannot sell. You should only become an agent for a long established direct selling company with saleable stock and a good track record.

How much can you earn?

Many people treat it as a secondary method of making money, and it should be treated that way until and if you become successful. Don't give up your job unless you are, and if you are unemployed it would be a bad mistake to think you can get out of trouble through this type of selling. You are unlikely to make a living wage at first. So be warned.

Marketing

Purely word of mouth and recommendation and introduction. Friends, and friends of friends, are likely to be your first port of call when you are on a recruitment drive.

Where to go for more information

You can get more information on direct selling and companies that require party planner organisers and reps from The Direct Selling Association.

The Direct Selling Association
29 Floral Street
London WC2E 9DP
071-497 1234

PET BOARDING

If you have a pet, and like domestic animals, you can earn a good living out of setting up kennels or a cattery.

Are you suitable?

Obviously you have to be responsible. Pets are like children: they need care and attention — and feeding! And you need a large, secure, and preferably green and rural area to set up your kennel or cattery.

How much can you make?

If you are successful you can make a very good living out of running kennels or a cattery. Charges for each animal can vary from about £4.00 to about £10.00 a day on average (depending on location and

facilities). For instance, if you have enough space for 50 dogs, that could mean as much as £500 a day and £3,500 a week — less all expenses.

Costs

Land, land and more land. The initial cost of land and suitable out-buildings to house cats or dogs are the major expense. But if you already have outbuildings and plenty of green space the costs can be kept to a minimum. Thereafter, feed is the only other day-to-day expense.

Regulations

Before doing anything, you have to gain planning permission from your local authority to build kennels or a cattery.

Under the Animal Boarding Establishments Act (1963), each local authority has the right to determine the materials used in the construction of kennels or a cattery.

You are required to be licensed under the provisions of the Animal Boarding Establishments Act if you provide boarding accommodation for animals. Licences are issued by your local authority. Details can be obtained from the Chief Environmental Health Officer of your council.

There are other Acts to be aware of, including the Dogs (Amendment) Act (1928), the Breeding of Dogs Act (1973), the Protection of Animals Act (1911) and the Guard Dogs Act (1975).

Where to find more information

When it comes to the construction and maintenance of boarding kennels, information can be obtained from the Animal Boarding Advisory Bureau, but note the other listed organisations for information and regulations.

The Animal Boarding Advisory Bureau
c/o Blue Grass Animal Hotel
Clatterwick Lane
Little Leigh
Nr Northwich
Cheshire
0606 891303

The Feline Advisory Bureau
Stonehenge Cats' Hotel
Orcheston
Nr Salisbury
Wiltshire
0980 620251

The Royal Society for the Prevention of Cruelty to Animals (RSPCA)
Causeway
Horsham
West Sussex
RH11 1HG
0403 264181

PHOTOGRAPHY

Are you suitable?

This could be the classic hobby-to-profession occupation. You obviously need to be interested in photography, and have practised since childhood, or for a long time.

Costs

Very expensive. You need a series of non-too-cheap cameras and accessories (zoom lenses and tripods); a dark room for processing black and white photographs — colour processing usually tends to go to specialist photographic processing labs — photoprocessing chemicals; and if yours is a studio based operation, a large studio, excellent lighting and photographic props.

Much of the equipment, though, can be bought secondhand through the photographic trade and amateur journals.

How much can you make?

How long is a piece of string? There really is no limit. If you are a top-notch advertising or editorial photographer used regularly by the advertising agencies, or top magazines and newspapers, you can earn tens of thousands of pounds a year.

If you are a leading freelance news photographer covering scandalous activity, celebrities or a war, you can earn a whole year's salary on one job alone by selling the rights through syndication so that your photographs are published throughout the world.

But that's the top end. Not everyone is a Lord Lichfield, David Bailey or Terry O'Neill. Most photographers eke out a crust by getting work when they can. Most photographers earn £100 plus for each assignment (around an hour's work or so). For most, child, portrait, and wedding photography will be easiest.

Qualifications

Learning on the job is the best form of tuition for aspiring photographers. Most photographers start as photographers' assistants to learn all the tricks of the trade and the basics. By working as an assistant you can learn to cope with clients and suppliers.

The overwhelming majority of photographers are self-employed and spend most of their time running their business rather than taking photographs.

You can get professional qualifications for photography — a BTEC (Business & Technician Education Council) HNC or HND, or a City and Guilds qualification.

Marketing

To get any work you have to get to the people who commission work — either PR agencies, marketing staff in firms, art and picture editors of magazines and newspapers.

A common way of securing business is to advertise in *Yellow Pages* and the Thomson directories, the various marketing and photographic annuals, and all the relevant user press, such as bridal magazines or the local paper.

You will need to produce a portfolio of your work to show just how good you are.

Pitfalls

You are only as good as your last job. The greatest problem with being a photographer is waiting for the next job — and these could be long periods without work. Don't let anyone down. That means reliable equipment, two rolls of film (at least) in case one does not come out, and reliable transport.

Where to find further information

The Association of Photographers represents the best of advertising, fashion, and editorial photography in the UK. The membership includes photographers' assistants, photographers' agents, photographic printers and photographers themselves. The AP publishes useful guidelines on becoming a photographer and a photographic assistant.

The Association of Photographers
9-10 Domingo Street
London EC1V 0TA
071-608 1441

The British Institute of Professional Photography (BIPP) is another important photography trade body.

The British Institute of Professional Photography
Fox Talbot House
Anwell End
Ware
Herts SG12 9HN
0920 464011

The National Union of Journalists is another body that news photographers and photo-journalists often belong to (they can then get a press card).

The National Union of Journalists
Acorn House
314 Gray's Inn Road
London WC1X 8DP
071-278 7916

PICTURE FRAMING

For all intents and purposes, picture framing is classed as a craft. It is a massive industry; everyone needs to have pictures framed at some time or another.

Are you suitable?

You need good judgement when it comes to matching frames with paintings. You also have to be good with your hands and have a good grounding in basic carpentry skills. Patience and care are needed to make frames fit perfectly.

Costs

Some picture framers work from retail outlets, others work from workshops, so the cost of renting either has to be taken into account.

On top of that you need a worktable, large shelves for storing paintings and glass, and you need all the basic tools to do the job, such as a mitre saw, clamps, rulers, stapling guns and a set square, as well as a good selection of lightweight and heavy hammers.

How much can you make?

You can make anything from £25 (labour and materials) per frame upwards. It really does depend on how expensive the frame is and the complexity of the framing process.

Market research

For your own education, you should go to public and commercial art galleries to gain an appreciation of why certain types of frame have been chosen for a particular painting and drawing. Check out local shops to see how many offer this service.

Marketing

Your market will be antique shops, art dealers, museums, professional artists, and the public.

To reach the public you must rely on recommendation, passing trade and advertisements in the local press. You could leaflet a particular neighbourhood, but the problem with this is that people only go to picture framers when they have a painting or drawing to frame.

When trying to attract custom from the business side, it is best to write to them, or place advertisements in trade and professional magazines.

PLANT CARE AND HIRE

If people go away for a two-week holiday in August and they have no one to look after their home for this period, their plants could die of thirst. Others may love having plants around the house, but are useless at looking after them. Or they may not particularly like plants, and so have very few, and yet for parties and other occasions they may think a splash of green may improve the surroundings. Where do they go? — to someone who can provide these services. And what about local businesses? Many need a plant hire and care service, don't they?

Are you suitable?

You need to have green fingers and a good knowledge of houseplant care.

Costs

You need a good van which you can allow to get messy, and a well-stocked glasshouse. Your raw material is plants, so in between jobs you have to keep tending to your stock and renewing it. You need a good selection of plants to choose from, and they have to be big to make an impact.

How much can you make?

As long as there is very little competition in your immediate area, you could do particularly well on the domestic front with the house plant care relief service. And on the businesses front you could do well if you are able to negotiate good contracts with service industries — PR consultancies, advertising agencies, financial services companies and firms of accountants, architects and solicitors, which normally have attractive offices and lobbies to impress clients. Plants blend in well with decor.

Market research

Find out if there are enough service companies in your area to approach. Find out what your competition would be, if any. The domestic market will be almost impossible to determine.

Marketing

You will need to offer a very good personal service to beat off any competition from larger firms, who may not even be based in your area. Dress smartly in a uniform with your business's logo when on jobs. Make yourself accommodating at all times. If a business (or domestic) client has a crisis, then try and see to them as soon as possible. At least if you are local, you can get round quicker than others could.

Send letters to all the likely businesses in your area that you think would benefit from your plant hire and care service. Send it to the office services or administrative manager if the firms have one. Then make arrangements to meet. Next, place advertisements in the local press, to attract custom from the public and businesses and 'small ads' sections of the office trade press (you can find them in your local library).

Remember, notices in local shops and newsagents may well attract local householders who may like your 'holiday relief' plant care service, and plant hire service. When visiting them, you will need to give them references, show them that you are trustworthy and reliable. They may well have already heard about you in vague terms through recommendation and word of mouth.

Pitfalls

Too much work to cope with.

Future

If you build up a very good local reputation, you will probably need to graduate from being a sole trader to a small business, with all the headaches that brings. You will then need more staff and more space elsewhere. You may find that you need to widen the area of your activity.

RENTING OUT ACCOMMODATION

If you have a good-sized home and some unused space, why not make money out of it? After all, your home is probably one of the biggest financial commitments you have ever made, and a major drain on your finances. However, it can also be a big money-spinner. It is not just a case of setting up office from home, but also using your home as a business.

Are you suitable?

Before reading on, you must decide whether or not you could bear to have anyone else living or staying in your home. If you cannot, forget these ideas. Your home should also be comfortable with all mod cons.

Renting a room

Taking in a lodger has long been a way for families to make ends meet. However, it is an even better money-spinner today because rent of up to £65 a week can be earned free of tax. Always check references from someone who is coming to share your home, take a deposit to cover damages, and check with your insurance company so that your household policy will not be invalidated. If the lodger runs off with your worldly goods you may find that you do not get a penny back from your insurance policy.

You do not have to get planning permission if you are merely taking in a lodger. However, if you have a house full of tenants you will need to comply with fire regulations. Check with your local planning department as you will probably have to apply for permission to convert your home or change its use.

However, you will not have to have planning permision if there are fewer than six people living together in a dwelling.

Bed and breakfast

This is another long-established way of earning a bit of extra cash on the side. B & Bs are the backbone of the tourist industry and tend to be family-run. The most important thing is to have the right location — a seaside resort or tourist spot are ideal.

Register your business with local tourist authorities to attract custom. Aim to get into guide books. However, remember that competition is tough and you will need to offer something special to make a living.

Check out what others offer in your area and what they charge. If you think you will need to modify your premises, make enquiries about local planning constraints and find out whether you will be able to finance your plans.

Contact your local tourist board for guidance on the potential demand. The Rural Development Commission and The Agricultural Development and Advisory Service will also be able to offer help and advice. All the relevant addresses and details of insurance, marketing and legal requirements is contained in a very useful guide from the English Tourist Board called *Starting A Bed And Breakfast Business*. Contact the British Tourist Authority for further details.

British Tourist Authority
Thames Tower
Black's Road
London
W6 9EL
081-846 9000

Guest houses

If you have a really large property you could turn it into a guest house and offer more than just bed and breakfast. Again, check with your local tourist authority for help and advice.

TEACHING ENGLISH AS A FOREIGN LANGUAGE

Are you suitable?

First, you need to like all nationalities. Second, you need to be pretty good at spoken and written English yourself. And lastly, you must be prepared for the frustration of teaching — so patience is a must.

Qualifications

There is no statutory need to have a qualification to teach English as a foreign language (TEFL), but it helps to get one. The course you could take is the Royal Society of Arts Preparatory Programme. There is also a more advanced course for those already with some teaching experience that takes eight weeks to complete. Special TEFL courses which relate to a particular subject like business English are also available.

There is no grant for the RSA preparatory course, and its cost is £500.

The market for TEFL

You can teach on a one-to-one basis from home, or as a tutor at one of the many technical colleges and foreign student colleges in and around London and the regions.

How much can you earn?

The rates in the UK range from £8–15 an hour.

Where to find more information

You should begin by writing to:

ARELS–FELCO (Association of Recognised English Language
–Federation of English Language Course Organisations),
2 Pontypool Place,
Valentine Place,
London SE1 8QF
071-242 3136

TELEWORKING

What is teleworking? Teleworking or telecommuting are both terms
that refer to the practice of working remotely from an employer, either
at home or at a telecottage. Advances in both computer and telecommunications technology have led to an increase in this way of working. Teleworkers come from all walks of life — from accountancy and
bookkeeping, to translation and data input. Even some BT directory
enquiry operators work from home, not that you would know that. But
they all have one thing in common. They want to work at or near
home rather than go through the turmoil of daily commuting, but they
need good telecommunications.

What is a telecottage or telecentre? It is a local centre that provides
low-cost access to information technology and telecommunications.
Users may be small businesses, community groups, or individuals who
work from home but need additional telecommunications and adminis-
tration support.

Are you suitable?

So, could this be the way you want to live your life? It could be if you
fulfil one of these three criteria:
- You want to be self-employed, and wish to work from home or
  near to home (and may need backup facilities supplied by a telecottage).
- You join a new employer who operates a teleworking policy.
- You convince an existing employer that you should be allowed to
  work from home.

Costs

If you are employed, then probably none. The employer will under-write the costs and still save money. If you are self-employed and use the facilities of a telecottage then you will have to pay a service charge.

Pitfalls

If you are not self-motivated and disciplined, then forget it — you have to be able to work well on your own. Working on your own, you also have to make sure you do not underwork (get tempted by distrac-tions), nor overwork — good time management is essential. Give your-self breaks, and make sure you limit the hours you work.

Where to find more information

There are now an estimated 600,000 self-employed teleworkers and 45 telecottages in the UK, and an association for you to join that promotes the concept of teleworkers, telecottages and telecentres, is the Telecottage Association.

The Telecottage Association
WREN Telecottage
Stoneleigh Park
Warwickshire
CV8 2RR
0203 696986

TOURIST GUIDE

Are you suitable?

Above all you need to be patient and understanding. Being a tourist guide can be taxing, particularly when you have to deal with questions in pidgin-English asked by foreign visitors.

You obviously need a basic understanding and working knowledge of the art, history, and architecture of the area or site you intend to 'work'.

A second, third or even fourth language would help providing you are reasonably fluent in them.

If you have these attributes, and you feel that this occupation is for you, then all you need to do is get yourself a qualification.

Qualifications

You need to take examinations to carry the badge of a qualified tourist guide. Although qualifications are not mandatory, you need them in London and the regions to gain admission into the principal tourist attractions.

The cost of the course

The cost of becoming a qualified tourist guide is approximately £600 plus VAT. You cannot get a grant for this training course. The course lasts six months or longer and at the end there is a three-hour exam and an all-day practical in which candidates are taken round by coach and examined verbally. Apply to your regional tourist board for full details.

The market for tourist guides

As a self-employed tourist guide your main market will be tour operators or as a guide attached to specific regional tourist boards. You can also work your own area or individual buildings. In London you can conduct themed walks — Jack the Ripper for instance — or become attached to particular sites such as the Tower of London or Hampton Court.

Most of the major regional tourist boards, including the London Tourist Board and Convention Bureau, produce a regular list of qualified guides (with all their particulars) and these are sent out to tour operators, travel agents, hotels and information centres.

Once a guide is registered with a tourist board, they can apply for membership of the Guild of Guide Lecturers.

How much can you make?

You usually get paid by the day or half day. Rates tend to be £45 for a half day and £65 for a full day. Although in London guides can earn a basic £92 a day.

Where to get more information

All the major regional tourist boards, and:

London Tourist Board and Convention Bureau
26 Grosvenor Gardens
Victoria
London SW1W 0DU
071-730 9367

Guild of Guide Lecturers
The Guild House
52D Borough High Street
London SE1 1XN
071-403 1115

TOYMAKING

So you liked playing with your dolls and train sets as a child? Why not have a career in making them?. And have you ever fancied making a hobby horse out of wood or inventing and producing a new teddy bear? Board games are very popular now, so if you have an idea for a game that would have universal appeal, you could be the next board game success story since four men from Canada invented Trivial Pursuit.

Are you suitable?

Toymaking is a mixture of having good hands, a creative mind, flair, and determination. If you have this combination of traits, then give it a try.

When you start, it is often a solitary job designing, making and marketing your toy or game. You may have to be a sole-trader by necessity, or you could go into partnership with someone who has complementary skills.

If you invent a game, then you will need persistence to get the game marketed. You will have to sell your game idea to a games manufacturer — the usual basis is that you earn royalties on sales.

Costs

Time is the biggest factor in toymaking. You could start by making very little money in the early days until you get well established. It is probably best that you start it off as a hobby. You will need some type of workshop, which can of course be in your home. And you will need all the tools and materials to make your toys — this could work out quite expensive.

If you are a games inventor, this should only be done as something in addition to your main job.

How much can you make?

This all depends on the type of toy you make, the demand for it and your own skills at carving out a niche in what is a very competitive market. If it is unusual, new or popular, then you could do very well indeed.

As a games inventor you could toil away for years and still get no rewards, but if you come up with a concept for a game that is unique, imaginative, and popular, then you could make millions.

Market research

Read the toy trade press (go to your library and sift through the publications). Browse through craft and toy shops, see what there is and ask the staff questions about what sells and what doesn't.

Marketing

You could sell your products off-the-page in trade publications, local and regional publications, and through 'small ads' in the national press and colour supplements. You could also sell your wares through toy wholesalers, agents, and small toy retailers. But your best shop window (and one which will act as a good test market) is toy fairs either locally, round the country, or held in London. These can cost a lot, so you could at first share a stand with other toymaking colleagues.

Regulations

If you specialise in teddy bears, wooden train sets or even hand-made jigsaw puzzles, don't forget to check health and safety regulations. Children's toys must be painted or treated with non-toxic finishes and cannot have any dangerous parts such as dolls' eyes that could fall out and be swallowed.

Members of the British Toy and Hobby Association are allowed to display the Lion Mark, which is a symbol of safety and quality. These toys are made to the BSI and EEC Toy Safety Directive: BS5665/EN71. The British Toymakers Guild publishes an information booklet entitled *EEC Toy Safety Directive 1990 — A Guide to Self-Certification.*

Where to find more information

If you are interested in developing a market for your toymaking, then it is wise to get in touch with the British Toymakers Guild with a view to possibly becoming a member of the Guild.

British Toymakers Guild
124 Walcot Street
Bath
Avon BA1 5BG
0225 442440

Or if you become involved in the manufacture of toys, games and playthings, then you could approach the much larger British Toy and Hobby Association. But you must: have a minimum turnover of £25,000 to join, have traded for at least a year, and have products which conform to BS5665/EN71.

The British Toy and Hobby Association
80 Camberwell Road
London SE5 0EG
071-701 7271

TYPING AND WORD PROCESSING

If you have skills as a typist these can be put to good use — either from your home, by temping, or working for someone else.

Qualifications

No formal ones are needed. However, you should be fast — or else you will not make money — accurate, and know how to present a document properly.

You can offer your skills to small firms which cannot afford their own full-time secretary, or need a bit of extra help. You can also contact local authors and colleges to offer to type up books, theses and reports.

Are you suitable?

If you are going to offer this service from home you must be prepared to spend hours typing at your personal computer, typewriter or word processor without much contact with anyone else. You must also be able to sell your service.

Cost

Very low, if you already have the equipment.

How much can you make?

This depends on how advanced your service is. Your best chances of making money are either to concentrate on a niche market or to offer other secretarial services. You can charge anything from £5 an hour — more for complex documents such as budget sheets.

WINDOW CLEANING

Got a bucket, rag, ladder and van? Right, you're in business. You can be a window cleaner. It's that simple!

Are you suitable?

You need a head for heights. Balancing on window ledges and climbing ladders to a height of a hundred feet or more is not everyone's cup of tea.

Costs

Just the cost of a long ladder or two and a lengthy van that you can mount the ladders on.

How much can you make?

If you are a go-getter and the area you are in is under-served by window cleaners (and believe it or not this is often the case), then you could make a lot of money as a sole-trader with just one assistant. If you service a few dozen homes a day at a few pounds a time the money soon adds up.

Market research

Check the areas you intend to work to see if many window cleaners work in the area. Knock on doors and ask residents if they need a window cleaner. That way you can gauge demand.

Marketing

Start doing a door-to-door round. It is the sort of trade where people will make an instant decision. Window cleaning is a chore that people do tend to put off. They can usually only be bothered to clean easy access windows and ones on the ground floor of a house. Also put cards in the windows of nearby shops and newsagents.

When your window cleaning business is seriously up and running, you can start leaflet-dropping and advertising in the local press.

Repeat business is important in this line of work, so try and sort out a rota, and ask customers how often they need their windows cleaned. That way, customers will be expecting you when you arrive; you will become as familiar as the milkman or postman.

Pitfalls

Bad weather can prevent you from working. No one wants to, or thinks about, hiring a window cleaner when it's raining or very cold. So be prepared for a slack period during the winter months. You may need to fall back on an alternative trade during this period of the year.

Future

If your window cleaning business is a roaring success you can take on staff, and stimulate more custom by advertising in the regional newspapers or radio, put a large advertisement in *Yellow Pages* or the Thomson directory.

Once you have a regular clientele in the domestic market, you can start writing and sending mailshots to local businesses and visiting them direct. And then you have a whole new market to tap!

WOOD-STRIPPING

Wood-stripping (or paint-stripping) has become a more popular activity during the last twenty years, as consumers have discovered the virtue of bare wood—pine and oak in particular—as part of the overall decorative effect of a home.

People like stripped pine doors and furniture; they feel it makes a home cosier, more rustic. Sir Terence Conran's Habitat stores set the trend in the 1960s and 1970s; stripped pine doors and furniture fitted in with the pine goods he sold to the nation.

Most woodstrippers use caustic soda-based products which are in fact alkaline, even though dipping is often called an 'acid bath'. You need a knowledge of types and ages of wood to know how long the wood needs to be dipped for. You can dip some hard woods as well as pine. Equipment can be bought from a hardware shop or builders merchant. Trimethylene chloride is used to hand-strip woods.

Are you suitable?

You have to be confident enough to handle an acid bath and dipping doors and other furniture in and out of the acid. You also have to bear the fumes, smells and mess that come with this job.

Costs

You need a suitable, but cheap, workshop or shop that is easily accessible from a road. The only other costs are for a suitable acid bath and chemicals.

How much can you make?

It is a bit of an up-and-down business. During recessionary periods people tend not to bother with wood-stripping so much, it is something they can live without. But you can make anything from £10 a door and more for larger or more intricate items of furniture like a chest of drawers or a wardrobe. You can charge more if an item is covered in several layers of paint and needs dipping several times.

Regulations

Check the planning and health and safety requirements with your local authority.

Market research

You have to site your business in an area which has a demand for this sort of service, such as conservation areas, and areas with streets and streets of old Georgian, Victorian and Edwardian houses. There would be very little demand for wood-stripping in a new town like Milton Keynes, but Hampstead in London is just the sort of area where you could make a good living.

You have to check out the competition. If there are three or four wood-stripping shops or workshops in a square mile area, then don't bother starting another one.

To find out about the types of woods that can be stripped and the length of time they should be dipped for, contact a supplier of the products.

Marketing

Cards in local shops, leaflet-dropping and advertising in the local press are very important ways of informing one and all of your new service.

Eventually, word of mouth and recommendations will be your best advertisement.

You could add value to your service if you were prepared to offer a pick-up and return service for items to be stripped. You charge extra for this door-to-door delivery service.

Why not offer waxing and varnishing as well? People hate varnishing, and particularly waxing, which is one of the most boring and laborious tasks around.

Future

Your premises could double-up as a second-hand shop for furniture or you could learn carpentry and furniture-making skills and build furniture to order or on 'spec'. These would be obvious extensions to your core business, and help level the peaks and troughs of the trade.

WRITING

Without doubt writing — of all types — is one of the most popular freelance and home-based activities. Journalism is the most common — writing feature articles and exclusive stories in the hope of selling them. You can also write fiction and try to sell your short stories or books to magazines or publishers. And, if you already have experience, you can become a copywriter writing punchy slogans and advertising and promotional literature for companies.

Pitfalls

It is often very hard to find work—writing, journalism and copywriting are very competitive. Even if you have talent it is not easy. You could end up starving in the proverbial garret for years before earning a penny. And if you want to enter the field of journalism you will need good contacts. It is a case of who you know, as much as what you know. However, if you stumble across an amazing story there is nothing to stop you ringing up a newspaper and offering to sell it to them.

Where to get more information

If you want information about training, careers and membership try:

The Institute of Journalists
2 Dock Offices
Surrey Quays Road

London
SE16 2XL
071-252 1187

The National Union of Journalists
Acorn House
314-320 Gray's Inn Road
London
WC1X 8DP
071-278 7916

The Society of Authors is the main trade body for writers and authors. It lobbies on behalf of its members and produces several useful publications: Quick Guides on Authors' Agents Copyright and Moral Rights; The Protection of Titles; Publishing Contracts; and several others. It also administers some of the main grants and writing prizes, including the Somerset Maugham Awards.

The Society of Authors
84 Drayton Gardens
London SW10 9SB
071-373 6642

Sources of further information

Association of British Factors and
   Discounters
1 Northumberland Avenue
London WC2N 5BW
071-930 9112

Association of Independent
   Businesses
26 Addison Place
London W11 4RS
071-371 1299

British Franchise Association
Franchise Chambers
Thames View
Newtown Road
Henley-on-Thames
Oxon RG9 1HG
0491 578050

British Technology Group
101 Newington Causeway
London SE1 6BU
071-403 6666

British Venture Capital Association
3 Catherine Place
London SW1E 6DX
071-233 5212

Business in the Community
8 Stratton Street
Mayfair
London W1X 5FD
071-629 1600

Chartered Institute of Patent Agents
Staple Inn Buildings
High Holborn
London WC1V 7PZ
071-405 9450

Data Protection Registrar
Wycliffe House
Water Lane
Wilmslow
Cheshire
SK9 5AF
0625 535777

Department of Education and
   Science
Sanctuary Building
Great Smith Street
London SW1P 3BT.
071-925 5000 [Helpline — 081-533
   2000)

Department of Employment
Caxton House
Tothill Street
London SW1H 9NF
071-273 6969 (Enquiries)

Department of the Environment
2 Marsham Street
London SW1P 3EB
071-276 0900

Department of Social Security
Skipton House

80 London Road
London SE1 6LW
071-972 2000

Department of Trade and Industry
Enquiry Unit
Room 131
131 Ashdown House
London SW1E 6RB
071-215 5000

Department of Trade and Industry
Small Firms Division
St. Mary House
c/o Moorfoot
S1 4PQ
0742 597531

Direct Selling Association
29 Floral Street
London WC2E 9DP
071-497 1234

Federation of Small Businesses
32 St Annes Road West
Lytham St. Annes
Lancs FY8 1NY
0253 720911

Finance and Leasing Association
18 Upper Grosvenor Street
London W1X 9PB
071-491 2783

Forum of Private Business
Ruskin Chambers
Drury Lane
Knutsford
Cheshire
WA1 6HA
0565 634467

HM Customs and Excise (VAT
    Advice Centre)
Dorset House
Stamford Street

London SE1 9PY
071-928 3344

Inland Revenue
Somerset House
The Strand
London WC2 1LB
071-438 6622

Institute of Chartered Accountants
Chartered Accountants Hall
Moorgate Place
London EC2P 2BJ
071-920 8100

Institute of Directors
116 Pall Mall
London SW1Y 5ED
071-839 1233

Institute of Patentees and Inventors
Suite 505a
Triumph House
189 Regent Street
London W1R 7WF
071-242 7812

Law Society
50-52 Chancery Lane
London WC2A 1SX
071-242 1222

Office of Fair Trading
Field House
Breams Buildings
London EC4A 1PR
071-242 2858

Market Research Society
15 Northburgh Street
London EC1V 0AH
071-490 4911

Patent Office
Cardiff Road
Newport
Gwent NP9 1RH

0633 814000

Prince's Youth Trust
5th Floor
5 Cleveland Place
London SW1Y 6JJ
071-321 6500

Registrar of Companies
Companies Registration Office
Crown Way
Maindy
Cardiff CF4 3UZ
0222 388588

Royal Institution of Chartered
    Surveyors
12 Great George Street
London WC2A 1SX
071-222 7000

Rural Development Commission
141 Castle Street
Salisbury
Wiltshire SP1 3TP
0722 336255

Small Business Bureau
46 Westminster Palace Gardens
Artillery Row
London SW1P 1RR
0276 452010

Further reading from Kogan Page

Do Your Own Bookkeeping, Max Pullen, 1988
The First 12 Months, Revised Edition, David H Bangs, 1993
Getting Started: How to Set up Your Own Business, 3rd Edition, Robson Rhodes, 1992
Going Freelance, 4th Edition, Godfrey Golzen, 1993
How to Make Money from Ideas and Inventions, R Rogers, 1992
Letting Residential Property, Frances Way, 1993
101 Ways to Start Your Own Business, Christine Ingham, 1992
Running Your Own Catering Company, Judy Ridgway, 1992
Running Your Own Mail Order Business, Malcolm Breckman, 1992
Running Your Own Market Stall, Dave J Hardwick, 1992
Technology Tools for Your Home Office, Peter Chatterton, 1992

Index of Advertisers